so easy… Home Sewing

25 fabulous items to make for your home

Caroline Smith

St Martin's Griffin
New York

www.stmartins.com

Illustrations and compilation by Carroll & Brown Limited 2006
Photography Jules Selmes, Roger Dixon
Projects developed and made by
Gwen Diamond, Cheryl Owen, and Caroline Smith

Library of Congress Cataloging-in-Publication Data Available Upon Request

ISBN-13: 978-0-312-35925-6
ISBN-10: 0-312-35925-X

First published in the United Kingdom by Carroll & Brown Publishers Limited

First U.S. Edition: September 2006

10 9 8 7 6 5 4 3 2 1

Reproduced in Singapore by Colourscan
Printed in China

Contents

Introduction 5

Fabric know-how 6

Equipment 8

Hand stitches 10

Sewing machine basics 12

Seams 16

Hems 18

Patterns and scaling 20

SIMPLE CUSHIONS 22

TABLE RUNNERS 24

TAB-TOP CURTAIN 26

TABLECLOTHS 28

BOLSTER CUSHION 30

Mitered corners 32

Buttons 34

Loops, ties, and tabs 36

Zippers 38

DUVET COVER 40

CUBE 42

ROLL-UP SHADE 44

CHILDREN'S TEPEE 46

POCKET STORAGE 48

Bias binding 50

Bias strips 52

Piping 54

CLOTHESPIN BAG 56

APRON 58

DIAPER STACKER 60

EYELET CURTAINS 62

Appliqué 64

Using trims 66

DUFFEL BAG 68

CAFE CURTAIN 70

MINI BEANBAG 72

TOTE BAG 74

Quilting techniques 76

PLACEMATS 78

OVEN MITTS 80

BEADED QUILTED THROW 82

PADDED HEADBOARD 84

LINED LINEN BASKET 86

BEACH ROLL 88

DINING CHAIR COVER 90

Fabric glossary 92

Index 96

Introduction

You'll be surprised by just how easy it is to get started making your own beautiful and desirable household furnishings and accessories. With an entry-level sewing machine, and your choice of fabrics and threads, you can create fashionable items for every room of your home and at a fraction of the store-bought price!

Possibly what's best about creating your own home soft furnishings is that you can ensure that they fit your specific needs, that they suit your home decor, and that you can have them as soon as you'd like.

This book begins with the basics – useful equipment, essential stitches, some general techniques, and a guide to hand and machine sewing. By this time you'll want to get on with your sewing, so there are a number of simple but effective projects to get you started, like some stripey cushions, a decorative table runner, and tab-top curtains.

Right from the beginning – and throughout the book – you will find the core techniques you will need to master to give your creations that professional look. Once a new technique – like sewing with bias binding – is introduced, a number of projects using it will follow.

As well as learning essential techniques such as how to miter corners in order to produce a flat edge, and how to put in a zipper, the book is filled with suggestions for making your items more decorative. There is information on appliqué, quilting, and applying ruffles and beads and other trimmings.

Because not everyone's taste or furniture is the same, many of the projects are accompanied by variations – padded covers that can suit both a rectangular and a shaped headboard, tablecloths for both round and rectangular tables, for example. And, there are Sew Smart tips scattered throughout that can help ensure a more perfect result.

You'll find a lot of satisfaction in creating your own home furnishings and you're certain to be the envy of your non-sewing friends. Some of the projects are suitable as gifts – presents for a house warming, new baby or a child's birthday or Christmas – which will be all the more appreciated because you've made them: Now all you've got to do is get sewing!

Caroline Smith

Fabric know-how

All of the projects in this book are accompanied by simple advice about the type of furnishing fabric you should use. This usually takes the form of a recommendation as to the weight of fabric you need – whether it's sheer, lightweight, mediumweight or heavyweight. You won't find your choice is limited – there is a huge range of different materials on sale within these weights. Generally speaking, dressmaking fabrics will be too fine for most of the projects.

When buying fabric, it's worth checking with the retailer as to its suitability for your project. He or she may also be able to advise you on how much fabric to buy, especially if you have chosen a material with a repeat pattern that may need matching up.

You also will need to find out about the care of your fabric – is it washable or does it need dry cleaning? Check, too, whether a washable fabric has been pre-shrunk – and if in doubt, wash the fabric before you use it. Most fabric is well labeled with this kind of information – just make sure that you take the information away with you.

SEW SMART
Right side or wrong side?
If your fabric looks the same on both sides, it is a good idea to try to use the same side throughout your project. Although they may look the same, there may be a subtle difference to the way each side catches the light, which may be more obvious after you've finished sewing. Make a small mark in an unobtrusive place, right on the edge of each piece that you cut out, to indicate what will be the wrong side for the purposes of your project.

Fabric amounts

Most of the projects in this book give you instructions on how to make up an item to a size that suits your specific needs. Therefore, you will have to measure up before you buy your fabric, and sometimes create your own pattern. You will be shown how to do this and how to use your measurements or pattern to cut out your fabric.

Bear in mind that most furnishing fabrics are 54–60" (135–150 cm) wide and are sold by the yard (meter). You will have to work out how many times the fabric pieces would fit across the width of your chosen fabric to determine how many yards (meters) you need. You also will need more fabric if you are trying to match a pattern across a piece. If the fabric you choose is an unusual width, sales staff can advise you as to the amount you need.

Cutting

You need first to line up edges and center lines with the grain of the fabric (see box). If you cut across the grain, you are cutting along the bias (any diagonal direction on the fabric) and the fabric will be stretchy. If you put two pieces of fabric together, say for a cushion cover, that haven't been cut out along the grain, they will pull in different directions as you stitch and the finished cover will be distorted.

When you cut out a square or rectangle, make sure you cut along the direction of the grain. If you cut out a circle, the true diameter should line up with the direction of the grain. If you are cutting out a shaped piece, then you need to find the vertical center line and match this to the grain.

So before you cut anything out, you will need to straighten the cross-wise grain and when you buy material, make sure you buy a bit more than you need to allow for these adjustments.

Straightening the ends

Before you begin, iron the fabric to get out any creases or folds. Snip into one selvage near the end of the fabric and pick out one or two weft (cross-wise) threads. Hold the fabric in one hand and pull at the threads with the other so the fabric gathers. Cut the threads free from the opposite selvage, then draw them out while pushing the fabric back at the same time. Cut along this line to straighten the end of the fabric. Repeat at the other end.

Re-aligning fabric

Fold the fabric in half lengthwise. Bring the selvages together and then check that the straightened edges line up. If any of the edges do not align correctly you need to re-align the grain. Fold the the fabric in half lengthwise and pin along the straightened edges, making sure they match. Bring the selvages together and pin. Spray or sponge the fabric with water until damp then stretch it along the bias, pulling it gently in both directions. Lay the material out on a flat surface to dry and then iron, if necessary.

If the fabric is distorted along the lengthwise edges, it may be simply that the selvages are too tight. All you need to do is to snip into the selvages at intervals.

Cutting surface

Always lay fabric out flat, ideally on a cutting mat placed on a table. This will give you a firm surface and cutting mats often have measurements marked on them that can be helpful. Alternatively, cover a table with a blanket; the fabric will grip the blanket slightly, making it easier for you to keep the material in position.

If you are cutting out anything particularly large, you may have to work on the floor. Again, put a blanket down first – this will also serve to protect your fabric from any dirt on the floor.

SEW SMART
Grain of fabric

The selvages are the fabric's finished edges. The lengthwise grain (warp) runs parallel to the selvages and has little give. The crosswise grain (weft) runs prependicular to the selvages and has a slight give. A fabric has its maximum give when it is cut on the bias, which runs at a 45° angle to the selvages.

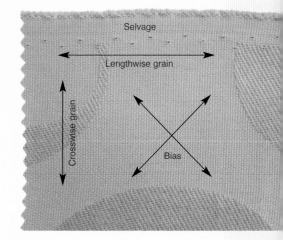

Selvage

Lengthwise grain

Crosswise grain

Bias

Equipment

Pins, needles, scissors, tape measure, and threads are essential to any sewing kit. Additionally there are a number of items, such as thimbles, bodkins, seam rippers, and pin cushions that will make any sewing project easier to achieve.

Pins and needles

Dressmaker's pins are most useful since they are suitable for nearly all fabrics. Those with colored ball heads are particularly handy since they are easier to see and pick up.

Most needle types come in different sizes, and are numbered accordingly. The lower the number, the thicker and shorter the needle. For most general sewing projects, use needles known as sharps. These are available in a range of different sizes to suit different fabrics. Generally speaking, the finer the fabric, the finer the needle you should use.

Thimble

This protects your fingers and is especially useful if you are working with a thick or stiff fabric, or are stitching through several layers.

Needle threader

If you experience difficulty when threading a needle, then this useful little tool is the answer. You simply insert the fine wire loop of the threader into the eye of the needle, pass the thread through the wire loop and then pull it back through the eye.

Pincushion

This is the perfect place to store your pins safely. Particularly useful are those with a wrist band, allowing you to keep pins close by while you work. Many come with a little emery bag attached. This is filled with an abrasive substance and you clean your pins and needles by pushing them inside.

Seam ripper

This is used for unpicking seams and cutting into buttonholes.

Bodkin

This is a long blunt needle-like tool with a large eye, useful for threading ribbon, tape, cord or elastic through a casing or row of eyelets. Some have two eyes or a safety-pin type closure to hold the ribbon securely.

THREADS

Different types of thread are available and you should choose a thread to match your fabric weight, color, and purpose. Use a thread that is darker or the same color as your fabric.

For general machine and hand sewing, general purpose cotton thread is ideal for cotton, rayon, and linen fabric. Mercerized means it has a smooth and silky finish. General purpose nylon thread can be used on light- to medium-weight synthetics.

You can buy special basting thread but it's more economical to use the ends of reels, especially if they are distinctive colors that you are less likely to use again. Don't be tempted to use cheap thread for basting – it will snap as you work and won't hold as firmly. Use a strong colored thread that's visible against whatever you are making, so it's easy to pick out when you've finished.

Tape measure

Essential for measuring, choose one with both inch and metric measures.

Shears and scissors

Ideally, you should have some large, dressmaker's shears for cutting out fabric. The handle of these scissors bends upward while the angle of the lower blade allows the fabric to lie flat during cutting. Pinking shears cut a zigzag edge that is excellent for finishing raw edges on fabric and which also can have a decorative use.

Smaller scissors are ideal for trimming seams and snipping into curves. A pair of embroidery scissors can also come in handy for general sewing – the small, thin blades can be useful for clipping, cutting buttonholes open and ripping seams.

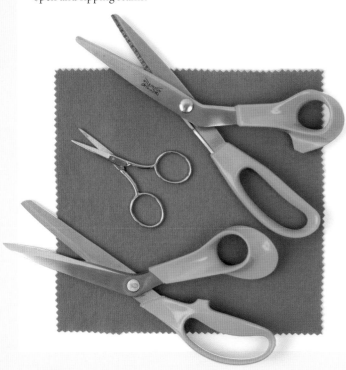

Hand stitches

Although most of the sewing you do will be with a sewing machine, very few projects won't require handstitching of some kind. You may simply need to use some basting to hold fabrics together more firmly than pins, or you might have to do some fine slipstitching to close an opening. Here are the hand stitches you are most likely to use.

Most, but not all, hand stitches are worked from right to left, although if you are left-handed you will want to reverse the working direction. Cut your thread with scissors to get a neat end that will make it easier to thread the needle.

Before you start stitching, secure the thread to the wrong side of the fabric. Tie a knot at the end of the thread; you might have to use a double or triple knot so it can't be pulled through the fabric. Alternatively, make several small stitches in one spot at the beginning of your stitching. When you finish, make a few small backstitches. If you are working a line of permanent stitching, secure the beginning and end of the thread where it won't be seen on the right side.

Basting

This is used to hold together temporarily pieces of fabric before final stitching. The more firmly you want your fabric held together, the smaller and neater your stitches should be. You can also use a line of basting – instead of a marker pen – to indicate a position on the fabric. Remove basting stitches at the end of a project; to avoid too much repetition, the instructions in this book will not mention this. You will only find references to removing basting when it's taken out before the end.

Running stitch

This is used for quilting, gathering, mending, and tucking. It's usually a permanent stitch.

Backstitch

Use this when you want a stitch that is particularly secure. It looks like machine stitching on the right side but the stitches overlap on the wrong side. You would also use backstitch at the end of a row of hand stitching to secure the thread.

Slipstitch

This is used when you need to make hand stitches that won't be seen. You make even slipstitches when joining two folded fabrics together and uneven slipstitches when joining a folded edge to a flat surface. It's useful for hemming and when you want to stitch an opening closed after turning an item to the right side.

Overhand stitch

These small even hand stitches are used when joining two finished edges together, such as when adding an edging or trim (pictured above). With right sides together, so one edge is at the back and one at the front, insert the needle diagonally from the back to the front, picking up only a couple of threads along each edge. Pull the thread through then insert the needle directly behind the point where the thread emerges for the next stitch.

Hem stitch

Hem stitch is a slanting stitch that is stronger than slipstitch. You can see the stitches on the wrong side but they are tiny on the right. If you don't want the stitches to be seen on the fabric or the hem, use slipstitch.

Catchstitch

This looks like the herringbone stitch that's used in embroidery. It is used on a hem where the edge of the turned fabric is pinked or finished with zigzag stitch. It's worked from left to right.

Blanket stitch

Though often used as an embroidery stitch, blanket stitch is used to finish the raw edge of an unfrayable fabric, like fleece or felt, and to hold a turning in place.

This stitch is worked from left to right on the right side, with the edge at the bottom.

11

1 Basting
Make short even stitches – about ¼"
(5 mm) long – the same distance apart.
Pass the needle in and out of the fabric
several times before you pull it through.

2 Running stitch
Similar to basting, but stitches are much
smaller and evenly sized and spaced.

3 Backstitch
Bring the needle to the right side and
insert it a half-stitch's length behind the
point where the thread emerges. Bring
the needle out again a half-stitch's length

in front of that point; pull the thread
through. For the next stitch, insert the
needle where the thread emerged for the
previous stitch and then bring the needle
out again a half-stitch's length in front;
continue. At the end, bring the needle to
the front where the thread emerges.

4 Slipstitch
To work along two folded edges, bring the
needle out through one edge and make a
stitch along the fold of the opposite edge.
Draw the thread through and make a stitch
in the opposite edge; continue. To work
along a folded edge and flat surface, bring

the needle out though the folded edge and
make a very small stitch in the flat fabric,
catching just a few threads with the needle.
Opposite this stitch, insert the needle in the
fold and take a small stitch along it, bring
the needle out and pull the thread through.
Continue alternating between the flat
surface and the folded edge.

5 Hem stitch
Bring the needle through to the front of the
fold. Pick up one or two threads from the
flat fabric and insert the needle through the
folded edge at the same time. Draw the
thread through; continue in this way.

6 Catchstitch
Bring the needle through the hem. Take
a very small stitch in the fabric above the
hem, just a little way to the right,
inserting the needle from right to left
and picking up only a couple of threads.
Take the next stitch in the hem, just a
little way to the right.

Blind catchstitch is worked in the
same way, but just under the edge of the
hem – you hold the edge back with a
finger as you work.

7 Blanket stitch
Secure the thread on the wrong side at
your starting point and bring it below
the edge. Insert the needle through the
fabric from the right side and down
toward the edge. Making sure the
thread is looped behind the needle, pull
in through to form the stitch on the
edge. Keep the depth of the stitches and
the distance between them even.

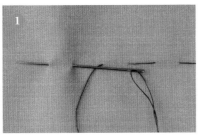

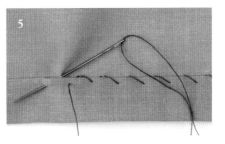

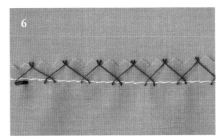

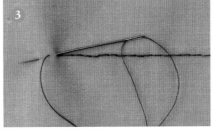

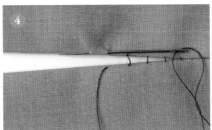

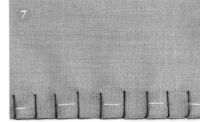

Sewing machine basics

For all but the smallest of tasks, a sewing machine is essential. The most advanced, top-of-the-range models offer a huge number of different stitches – upward of 50 – and allow you to perform many functions. They are often computerized, with built-in memories where you can store your embroidery stitch designs. However, even the most basic models provide a great range of functions – you can do buttonholes, sew in zippers and piping, stitch stretch fabrics, as well as working with the basic straight and zigzag stitches.

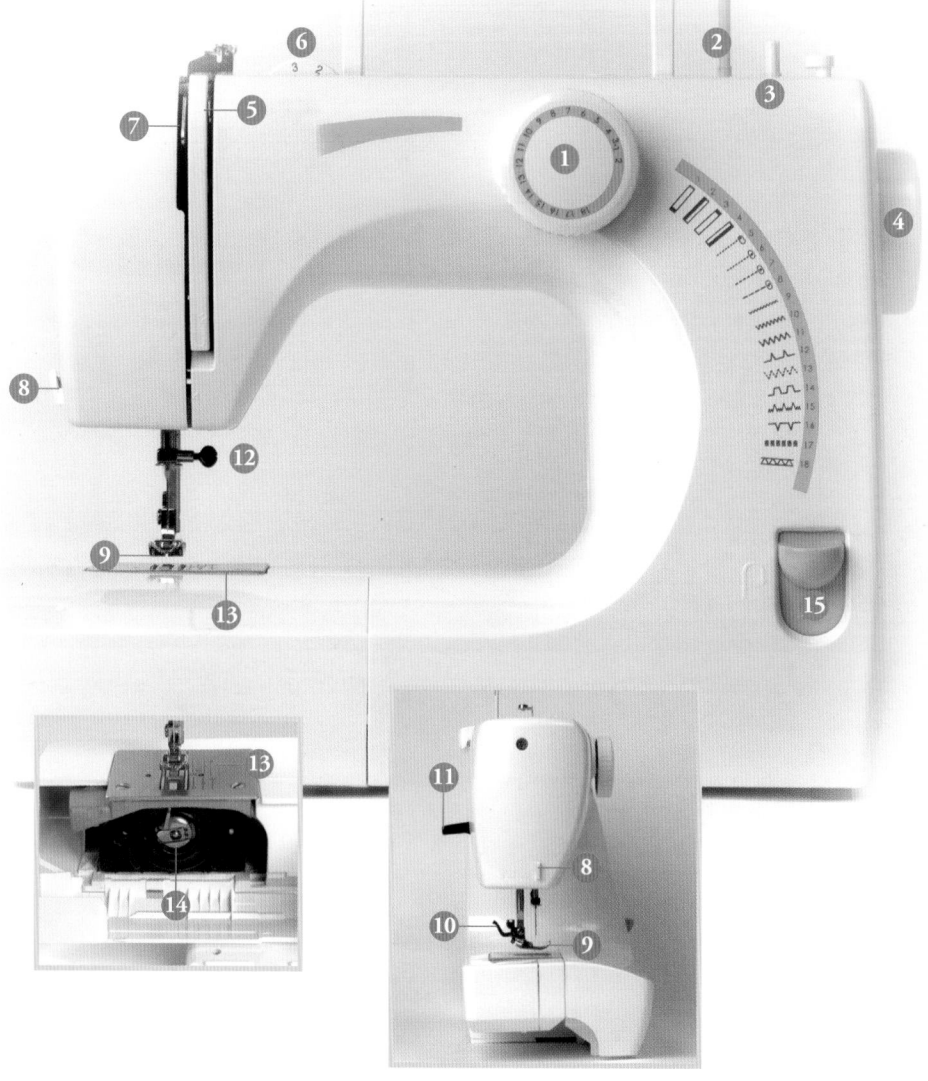

All the projects in this book have been completed using a fairly simple, standard sewing machine and a couple of attachments. All you need is a machine that does straight and zigzag stitching, makes buttonholes, and has a zipper foot. A useful optional extra is an even-feed (or walking) foot (see page 15), especially if you make up anything that is quilted. It is worth making sure that your machine can sew heavy fabrics, as some lightweight models can't be used with the thicker upholstery materials.

All machines operate on the same principle. Basically, a sewing machine works with two threads, a top thread and a bottom thread. The bottom thread is wound around a bobbin that is inserted inside the machine, under the needle. As you sew, the needle pierces the fabric and takes the top thread down to the bobbin. The top thread loops round the bobbin and picks up the bottom thread, pulling it up into the fabric. So the two threads interlock to create the stitching.

Most sewing machines are threaded in a fairly similar way and use similar controls to adjust important features such as tension and stitch length. You will find that once you learn how to thread and use one model, you will probably be able to apply that skill to almost any other machine.

These pages are intended as a general guide only and you will find that the positioning of certain features will differ from machine to machine. You should rely on the manual for your particular model.

1 Stitch length/type selector – This allows you to select both the size and type of stitch. Some machines have separate stitch length and type controls, and others also have stitch width selectors for zigzag or fancy stitches.

2 Spool pin – Place your reel of thread on the spool pin before threading the machine. Some models come with an attachment to hold the reel in place.

3 Bobbin winder – This is the spool on which you place the bobbin for winding. The reel of thread is placed on the spool pin, the thread is passed through a thread guide (refer to your manual) before being wound around the bobbin a few times. The bobbin is placed on the winder and then the needle is disengaged – this is often done by simply moving a switch, or by loosening the flywheel (refer to your manual). Then, when you press the foot pedal, the bobbin will wind. Make sure the thread winds evenly on to the bobbin and always use the same thread that you are using for the top thread.

4 Handwheel – Modern electric machines are operated by means of a foot pedal. However, they still have a handwheel so you can control the needle without using the pedal. It means you can stitch slowly, if necessary, and you can raise or lower the needle as required.

5 Tension guide – The top thread passes through two discs, which exert pressure on the thread. The more pressure, the tighter the tension on the thread. Lower pressure and you'll have looser thread (see page 14).

6 Tension settings – This adjusts the tension that helps control the flow of the top thread.

7 Take-up lever – The top thread is passed through the take-up lever after being passed round the tension discs. It rises and falls with the needle: When the take-up lever is at its highest point, so is the needle.

8 Thread cutter – when you've finished sewing, pull the thread over the cutter to cut it. The position of a thread cutter varies, if present, but it will be somewhere near the needle.

9 Presser foot – This presses down on the fabric to hold it in place, and works with the feed to move the fabric through as you sew. When it's lowered, it engages the tension discs, so to thread the machine, you need to have the foot raised. The foot may be changed, depending on the task (see below).

10 Presser foot clamp – This is released (or unscrewed) to remove the presser foot.

11 Presser foot lever – This lever, usually at the back of the machine, is raised or lowered to raise or lower the presser foot.

12 Needle clamp – This is released to remove the needle. When changing needles, always replace them correctly or the machine won't work. Refer to the manufacturer's manual for instructions.

13 Throat plate/feed – The throat plate lies under the needle; the feed is the metal teeth that emerge through openings in this plate. When the sewing needle goes down into the machine to pick up the bobbin thread, it passes through a hole in the throat plate. The feed works with the pressure of the presser foot to move the fabric along and get it in the right position for each stitch.

14 Bobbin case – Once a bobbin has been wound, it goes into the bobbin case. The type of bobbin case varies. Some are located under a removable plate, beside the needle plate, and you simply drop the bobbin in place. With other models, the bobbin is held in place with a small latch or it can be accessed from the front of the machine and then removed. The bobbin is then slipped into the case and the thread passed through the relevant notches before the case is returned to the machine.

15 Reverse switch – By depressing this, the machine will stitch backward. This is used when you want to secure the stitching at the beginning and end of a seam.

Getting started

First, wind the thread on to the bobbin then thread the machine. Raise the presser foot then turn the handwheel so the take-up lever is in its highest position. Put a reel of thread on the spool pin. Take the thread across the machine to the first thread guide, then down to the tension guide. Take it up to the take-up lever – some of these have an eye for the thread or a simple slot. Then take the thread down toward the needle, passing it through any thread guides. Thread the needle in the direction indicated by your machine's manual. If it is not in the correct direction, the machine won't work.

Insert the bobbin in the bobbin case, following your manual's instructions, making sure there is about 6" (15 cm) of thread emerging from the bobbin. Leave the plate or covering open so you can see the bobbin. Turn the handwheel so the needle moves down and then up again to its highest position. As the needle comes up you will see that the top thread has picked up a loop of the bottom thread. Use a pin and pull the loop through so the bottom thread is now on the outside of the machine. Close the plate or cover to conceal the bobbin.

Sewing

Before starting your work, try out your stitching first on a scrap of the same fabric in order to get the stitch length and tension right. Choose your stitch and select a length (see page 15). Fold the scrap in half to work through two layers. Use the handwheel to lift up the needle to its highest point. Make sure the presser foot is raised. Place the fabric under the needle, with the bulk of the fabric to the left. Lower the presser foot and turn the handwheel to bring the needle down into the fabric. Make sure the tension setting is at its mid point. Press the foot pedal to start sewing. Use your hands to lightly guide the fabric through – never pull – but keep your fingers away from the needle. Stitch for a short distance.

When you've finished, raise the presser foot and turn the handwheel to raise the needle. Draw the fabric away from the machine and use the integral cutter or scissors to cut the threads free, leaving about 6" (15 cm) of thread loose.

Finishing

To secure the thread ends at the ends so the stitches don't unravel, use the reverse stitch function on your machine. When you start stitching, position the needle just in from the beginning of your seam. Hold down

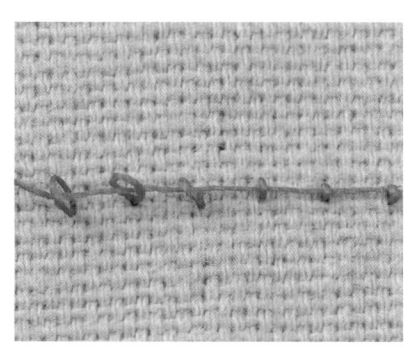

Correct tension
The top and bottom threads should lay flat on the surfaces.

Incorrect tension
When either the top or bottom thread is too loose, you will get this result.

the reverse and stitch back to the beginning. Release the reverse and then stitch forward to the end of your seam. Now hold down the reverse again and stitch backwards for a few stitches.

Correcting tension

If the tension is just right, the point where the top and bottom threads interlock will be midway between the two layers of fabric, and the stitching will look the same on both sides.

If, however, the bottom thread appears on the top of the fabric then the tension for the top thread is too tight. To correct this, turn the tension setting to a lower number (or toward the minus range on some machines)

and then do another test. If the top thread appears on the bottom of the fabric then the tension of the top thread is too loose. Turn the tension setting to a higher number (or toward the plus range) and test again.

It is always preferable to adjust the top thread tension if the stitching is not right. While the bobbin tension can be changed on most machines, it is a fiddly job and you wouldn't want to do it every time you changed fabrics. Usually you have to tighten or loosen a small screw on the bobbin case. Refer to your manual before attempting this – and only adjust bobbin tension as a last resort.

Stitch length

Match your stitches to your fabric – use short stitches for fine fabrics and long ones for heavyweights. Generally speaking, the lower the number on your stitch length selector, the longer the stitches – although you should refer to your manual. If you use stitches that are too small, the fabric will pucker and you will find it hard to get the tension right. If the stitches are too long, they will be too loose and may pull out. Check the stitch length when you test the tension (see page 14).

Sewing machine needles

Needles for sewing machines are made in different sizes; the lower the number the finer the needle. Commonly available sizes range from 9 to 18. Match the needle to your project; for a fine, sheer fabric, you need a fine needle, such as size 9 or 10. Needles also vary in the type of point. Most projects use regular, sharp-pointed needles, but if you're stitching a knit fabric use a ball-point needle. You also can get wedge-point needles specially designed for leather, suede or vinyls.

Sewing-machine feet

Different kinds of sewing-machine feet allow you to work on a range of projects. You can get feet that will help you to sew on beads or sequins, to do appliqué or to make ruffles. The following will be the most useful for the projects in this book.

• **Multipurpose foot (A)** Your sewing machine will probably come with one of these, which is used for straight and zigzag stitch. It can be known as a zigzag foot.

• **Straight stitch foot** – Your machine may use specific feet for straight and zigzag stitches so this foot can only be used for straight stitch.

• **Zipper foot** (B) Use this when you want to stitch along the side of something bulky. It's used, obviously, when inserting zippers, but can also be used to stitch piping in place, or when covering cord to make your own piping. You can fix it so the needle passes to either the right or the left of the foot, depending on your needs.

• **Buttonhole foot** (C) Most machines come with this attachment, which allows you work the stitching for a buttonhole in just four steps. A gauge on the foot helps you to work even buttonholes.

• **Even-feed foot** This feeds layers of fabric through the machine at an even rate. It's useful for any bulky, slippery, or stretchy fabrics and for quilting, when it may be combined with a quilting guide attachment that helps you to work parallel lines.

Machine stitches

1 Straight stitch

The basic machine stitch, it is formed by two interlocking threads and looks the same on the front and back. The length of the stitches can be changed to suit the fabric (see Stitch length, left).

2 Topstitch

This is used on the right side of the fabric for decorative as well as functional purposes. When you've stitched two layers of fabric together and turned them to the right side, topstitching around the edges helps them lie flat. It also can give turnings a neater finish.

3 Zigzag stitch

Often worked along the raw edge of fabric, at seams, and on turnings, most machines offer this stitch. By working it close to the edge, it forms an overcast stitch.

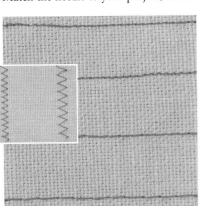

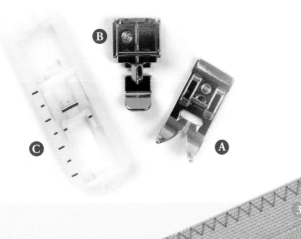

3   1   2

The most basic seam is formed when you use a straight machine stitch to sew two pieces of fabric together. This plain seam is the most commonly used and is suitable for many different purposes.

When you stitch two pieces of fabric together, the distance between your line of stitching and the edge is the seam allowance. When the seam has been finished, that area is then referred to as the allowance. The most common seam allowance is ⅝" (1.5 cm) wide, but this can vary depending on your project. It is important to use allowances — if you aren't consistent, you will find that the pieces don't match up correctly when you are putting a project together. To stitch a plain seam, pin your fabric together and machine stitch along the edge of the fabric, keeping to the seam allowance.

If you have stitched a seam that goes around a sharp corner, you will need to trim the allowance at this point to reduce the bulk of the fabric when you turn the finished seam. If you have stitched a curved seam you need to make small cuts in the seam to get a neat finish when turned to the right side. And if you think the raw edges of your seam are likely to unravel, you can finish them in a variety of ways.

SEW SMART

Turning to the right side

If you need to leave a gap in a seam in order to turn an item to the right side, when you get to the point where you want to start stitching, stop stitching. Then stitch backward for a short interval. Draw the fabric out of the machine and cut the threads. Reposition the fabric in the sewing machine a short interval in front of where you want the seam to start again. Stitch backward to that point and then stitch forward to complete the seam.

When you've finished stitching, finish the seam as necessary and turn the item through the gap to the other side. Push a knitting needle gently into any corners to get a neater finish. Press the allowance under on both sides of the gap and then slipstitch (see page 11) it closed.

Finishing plain seams

Pinked finish This is the simplest finish for the edges of a seam. Use the pinking shears to trim along the edges of the allowance.

Pinked and stitched finish (1) Stitch along each seam allowance ¼" (6 mm) in from the edge. Then trim the edge with pinking shears.

Turned and stitched finish Turn under the edge of each seam allowance by ¼" (6 mm) and press. Stitch along the edge of the fold.

Zigzagged edges Set the machine to zigzag and stitch along each seam allowance, close to, but not on, the edge.

Then trim close to the stitching. Sometimes you will want to stitch the seam allowance together using zigzag stitch – this reinforces the seam at the same time as neatening the edges.

Bound edges Fold binding over each seam allowance and then secure with topstitching (see page 15).

Self-finished seams

There are some seams where the raw edges are enclosed within the seam, so avoiding the need for finishing.

French seam (2) Pin your fabric wrong sides together. Stitch, taking a ¼" (6 mm) allowance. Press the seam to one side. Turn the fabric so the right sides are together and pin along the seam again, making sure the stitching is exactly on the edge. Stitch again

⅜" (1 cm) from the folded edge, so the first seam is enclosed; press the seam to one side.

Mock French seam Pin the fabric right sides together. Stitch, taking a ⅝" (1.5 cm) allowance,. Turn in each allowance by ¼" (6 mm) and press. Pin the turned edges together and stitch, close to the fold. Press the seam to one side.

Flat fell seam (see detail on page 16) This seam lies flat and is held in place with topstitching, that shows on the right side. Pin the fabric right sides together. Stitch taking a ⅝" (1.5 cm) allowance. Trim one of the allowances to ¼" (6 mm). Fold the other allowance over the trimmed one and press. Pin the allowance flat on the fabric so the trimmed seam is underneath. Topstitch through all the layers.

Topstitched seams

These are a good way to hold seams flat, and so also help prevent unraveling of raw edges. If you are planning on using topstitching elsewhere in your project, consider using this kind of seam.

Double topstitched (3) Stitch a plain seam with a ⅝" (1.5 cm) allowance and press the seam open. Topstitch ¼–⅜" (6 mm–1 cm) from the seam on the right side, so you are stitching through the fabric and allowance. Turn and topstitch down the other side of the seam, keeping to the same distance.

HAND FINISHING
Seams on lightweight fabrics that don't fray easily can be finished with handstitching. First, press the seam open then trim one allowance to ⅛" (3 mm). Turn the edge of the other seam allowance under ⅛" (3 mm) and press. Turn again, bringing it to the seamline so that it encloses the trimmed edge. Press, then hemstitch as close to the first line of stitching as possible.

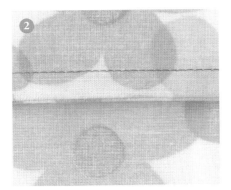

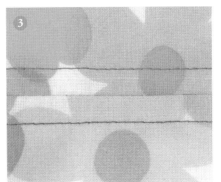

Hems

Hemming is used to finish the raw edges of fabric by folding it out of sight. When you are instructed to turn under a hem, you need to fold the fabric to the wrong side. If you turn under the fabric once, you make a single hem. Turn the fabric under twice and you have a double hem.

You can hold a hem in place with stitching that is either visible or invisible. Machine stitching along a hem is the simplest way and it will be very secure. However, the stitching will be visible on the right side. Alternatively, you can use one of the variety of hand stitches that catch up only a few threads of your fabric and that are barely visible on the right side. You also can make a feature of a hem and use means of securing it in place that will serve a decorative purpose.

A hand-rolled hem should be used on very fine or sheer fabrics where a flat turned hem would show through the fabric.

A blanket-stitch hem gives a decorative edge at the same time as hemming fabric. It looks particularly good stitched with darning wool or embroidery thread on fabrics with a thick pile, such as fleece and felt, where the stitches sink into the raised surface of the fabric. As the name suggests, it is the traditional finish for the edge of blankets.

If you are hemming a square or rectangular item, such as a napkin or tablecloth, you will come to a corner. You can simply fold under one hem first, and then fold the next one over the top of the first. This will, however, be bulky since you are folding several layers of fabric into each corner. The neatest way to deal with corners is to fold them into miters (see page 32). Since you cut away excess fabric with this method, the corners should lie flat and neat.

Sewing a hem

Basic single hem

In both these versions, the raw edge of the hem has been pinked and stitched (see page 17).

1 Machine stitched

Finish the raw edge of the fabric. Turn under the edge by ⅝" (1.5 cm) and press. Machine stitch on the wrong side, close to the first stitching.

2 Hand stitched

Finish and turn the edge of the fabric as above. Use catchstitch (see page 11) to sew along the edge, making your stitches in the hem just below the pinking or zigzag.

Basic double hem

3 Machine stitched

Turn under the fabric by ⅜" (1 cm) and press. Turn it under again by ⅝" (1.5 cm) and press again. Machine stitch on the wrong side, close to the first fold you made.

4 Hand stitched

Turn under the fabric as above and pin along the hem to hold it in place. Use hem stitch or slipstitch (see page 11) along the first fold you made.

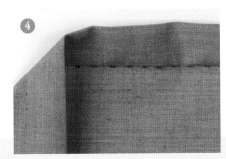

Hand-rolled hem

Machine stitch ⅜" (1 cm) from the edge of the fabric, then trim the fabric close to the line of stitching. Turn under a hem so this line of stitching is close to the fold on the wrong side. Secure the thread at the right-hand side and take a small stitch in the fold, just outside the stitching. Take the next stitch in the fabric, ¼" (5 mm) from the fold. Continue in this way until you've made about five stitches in both the fold and the fabric. Pull up the thread to roll up the hem. Continue stitching for short intervals and then pulling the thread.

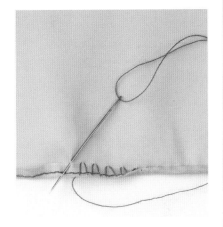

Blanket-stitched hem

Turn under a single or double hem and pin it in place. Secure the thread under the hem on the right-hand side and bring the needle out on the very edge. Turn to the right side and work blanket stitch (see page 11) along the hem, making sure the vertical stitches are the same depth as the turning.

Patterns and scaling

Because the items in this book will be made to individual measurements, there are few general patterns. Instead, you will be instructed to create your own patterns, based on your own requirements. However, the book does contain a few patterns, and these must be scaled up or enlarged for use. The easiest way to do this is to use a photocopier.

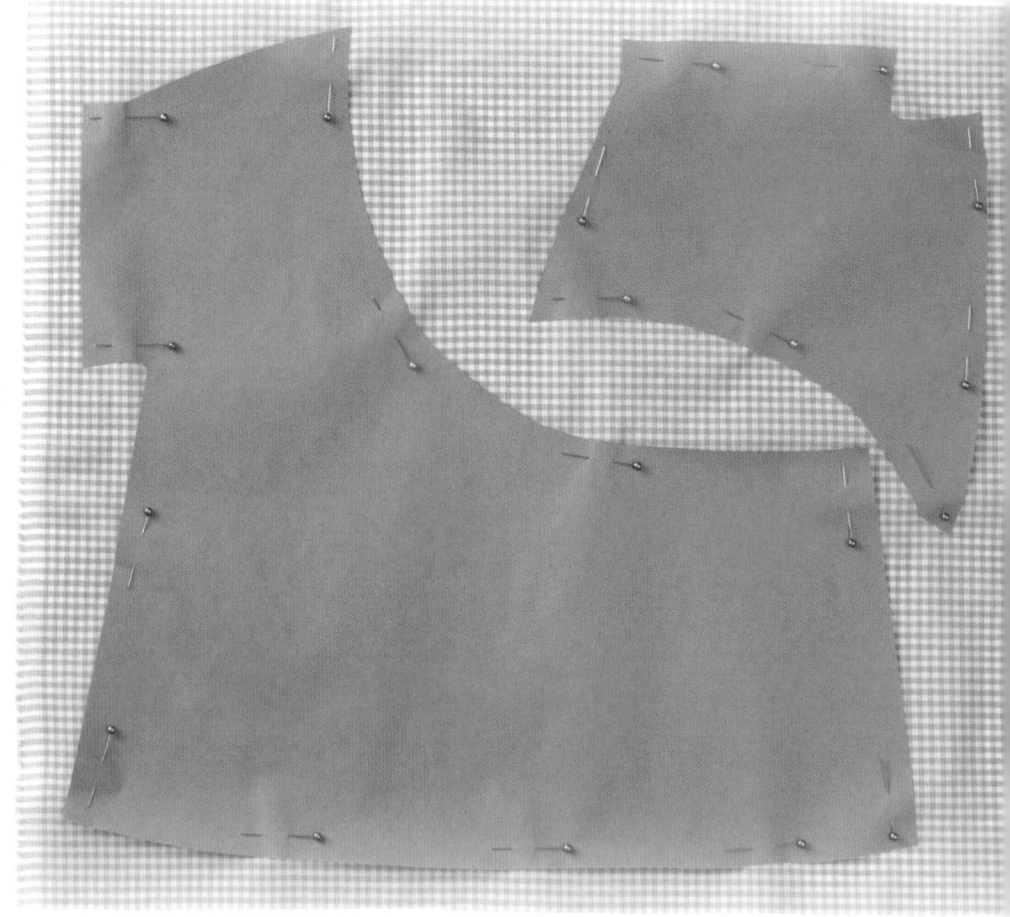

You should use an inexpensive but sturdy plain paper for cutting the patterns in this book. You may want to use the patterns again so its important that the paper won't deteriorate with handling. However, avoid stiff paper since it will be hard to pin to the fabric without it buckling. You may have to join several pieces of paper together if the pattern dimensions exceed those of the paper. Do not use newspaper, which can leave marks on fabric.

A ruler and pencil are vital for creating many of the patterns used in this book. Use an ordinary HB pencil that doesn't smudge so as to prevent marks transferring to your fabric. It can also be useful to have a set square or protractor for getting right angles right when drawing squares or rectangles. As you draw, make sure the line is clear enough to cut around later.

Some of patterns may have marks that need to be transferred to the fabric – these marks will help you line up the various sections of a make when putting them together. Use an erasable marker to do this.

If you are going to scale up a pattern, the easiest way is to photocopy the pieces, enlarging them to the right size (see below).

It's important to ensure that you position the pattern correctly on your fabric before you cut around it. You neeed to make sure that the pattern follows the grain of the fabric (see page 9). If you position the pattern any old how, your cut pieces will have a bias stretch and may become distorted when you come to sew them together.

When pinning the pattern to the fabric, using lots of pins will cause the pattern to wrinkle while too few pins will allow the pattern to move while you are cutting.

Enlarging a design

Take the scaled-down pattern and enlarge it on a photocopier until it is the right size. On the printed pattern for the clothespin bag (see page 56), for example, the longest back measurement is 2" (5 cm) while the finished pattern needs to be just over 16 " (40 cm) long. Photocopy the printed pattern, enlarging it by 200 percent – it's now 4" (10 cm) long. Then take the copy and enlarge that by 200 percent – it's now 8" (20 cm) long. Enlarge that copy again to get the final length – you will have to print out on A3 paper at this stage. Use this technique to scale up other patterns, although you may have to work out the percentage of the enlargement to get the correct size.

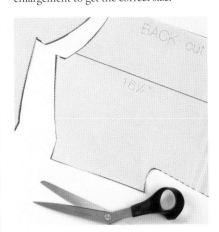

Making curves

To draw a large curve, take a length of string and attach it to the center point of one long edge of the fabric with a pin. Tie a pen to the other end, making sure the distance between pin and pen is the required radius. Keeping the string taut, draw the curve.

You also can use a circular object, such as a plate, saucer, or cup to round off an edge. If you want a large sweeping curve use a large plate. If you want a sharper, smaller curve, use a cup.

Lay the paper out flat and place the plate in the corner you want to round off. Move the plate until its edges touch the straight edges of the paper. Draw around the curve and then cut away the unwanted paper.

Using a pattern

Lay your fabric out flat and place the pattern(s) on top, positioning it so as to get the most out of the available fabric. If the pattern has a straight edge, line this up with either the lengthwise or crosswise grain. If it doesn't have straight lines but is symmetrical, fold it in half and run your finger along the crease to make a prominent fold line. Place the unfolded pattern on the fabric so the fold line is roughly lined up with the grain. Pin one end of the fold line in place and measure from this to the edge of the fabric (if this is not the selvage, make sure the edge is perfecly straight). Measure from the other end of the fold line to the selvage and adjust the pattern so the second measurement is equal to the first.

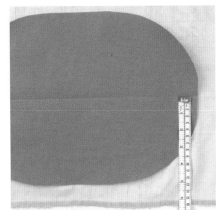

Cutting out

Pin around the outside of the pattern so it lies as flat as possible. Cut through the fabric toward the pattern. Rest one hand lightly on the pattern and cut around it. If an allowance has been included, cut close to the paper's edge. If you have to add an allowance, cut around the pattern the given measurement from the paper's edge. If you like, mark the fabric to indicate the allowance. If you have to cut out more than one piece of a pattern, either fold the fabric in half or put two layers together before you pin the pattern in place. If you are putting two layers together, make sure their grains line up with each other first. Then cut around the pattern, through both layers.

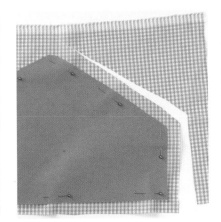

22 SIMPLE CUSHIONS

It's so easy to make your own cushion covers, and this design, with its overlapped opening at the back, is simplicity itself. The cushion form is inserted through the opening and then tucked under the overlap. By making the cover slightly smaller than the form, you end up with a puffier cushion.

You can use almost any fabric to make this type of cushion. If you plan to sit directly on the cushion then it's best to choose a mediumweight fabric. But if you're making scatter cushions for your bed or sofa, you also could use a lighter weight material. Alternatively, if you've got a heavyweight piece of fabric that you particularly want to make into a cushion cover, then use this for the front panel and a lighter material for the back panels. This cover is removable and so can be cleaned separately from the cushion form; if your cushion is going to get a lot of wear, then pick a washable fabric.

Once you have mastered the basic technique, you could add piping, tassels, or fringing before making up the final cover.

YOU WILL NEED

• Fabric – for amount see below

• Square cushion form

• Matching thread

23 Making up

Measure your cushion form and cut out one piece of fabric to the same size; this is for the front panel. For the back panel, cut out a piece of fabric that is 8" (20 cm) longer. Fold this into thirds widthwise and press. Cut along one of the folds to produce two pieces – the larger should be twice the size of the smaller. Mark the cut edges with pins.

1 Turn under each of the two marked edges, ¼" (5 mm), then 1½" (4 cm); press. Pin and topstitch both hems in place.

2 Pin the back pieces to the front, right sides together, matching raw edges and making sure that the hemmed edges overlap. Stitch around the sides, taking a ⅝" (1.5 cm) seam allowance. Stitch a second line of stitching just inside the first, at the side where the back panels overlap, for extra strength.

3 Snip across each corner to reduce the bulk and make a neater finish.

4 Finish the raw edges with zigzag stitch to neaten and prevent fraying. Turn the cushion cover to the right side through the opening and press. Insert the cushion form.

SEW SMART
The fabric for this cover is cut to the same size as the cushion form so that the finished cover is slightly smaller than the form. This gives the cushion a more puffy look when the form is in place. It works with this kind of cover since there is no closure, like a zipper or buttons, that would be strained by a tight fit.

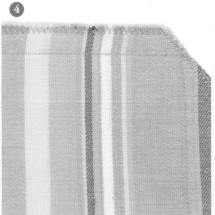

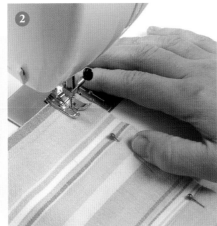

TABLE RUNNERS

Laid along the length of the table, a runner can help protect the surface when hot dishes are placed on top. It can be laid on a bare table or on top of a complementary cloth and teamed with matching mats and napkins for a coordinated table setting.

Below are instructions on making a reversible runner – the same material is used for both front and back. However, you could use a different fabric for each side, or a cheaper, plain lining as the backing material. If the runner will get a lot of use, choose a washable fabric.

YOU WILL NEED

• Main fabric – for amount see below

• Backing fabric (optional) – for amount see below

• Basting and matching thread

• Two tassels (optional)

• Paper, pencil, and ruler (for pattern)

Basic table runner

Determine the length of the runner – the length of the table plus any drops at either end – then add 1¼" (3 cm) for seam allowances. Decide on the finished width of the runner and add 1¼" (3 cm). Cut two pieces of light- or mediumweight main fabric to these measurements. (Alternatively, cut one piece of main fabric and one piece of backing material.)

1 Pin the two pieces of fabric right sides together. Stitch all around, taking a ⅝" (1.5 cm) seam allowance and leaving an 8–10" (20–25 cm) gap in one long side. Trim the fabric at the seams to ⅜" (1 cm) and snip across the corners. Neaten raw edges with zigzag stitch.

2 Turn to the right side through the opening then slipstitch the opening closed. Press, then topstitch all around, ⅝" (1.5 cm) in from the edge.

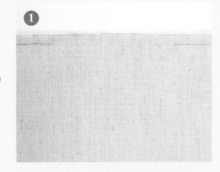

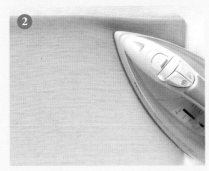

Table runner with shaped ends

This version has been given pointed ends. Experiment with other shapes, too.

1 Measure the table and decide how much drop you want at each end, including the area that will be shaped. Decide on the width. Add extra for seam allowances, as before, and cut out two pieces of fabric. Make a pattern for the shaped end (see Patterns and scaling, pages 20–21) and pin this to one end of one piece. Cut around the pattern then repeat at the other ends of the fabric.

2 Pin both pieces of fabric right sides together and stitch as in step 1 of Basic table runner (left). Trim and neaten the seams as before, making sure you snip off any excess at points. Finish off as in step 2 of the Basic runner.

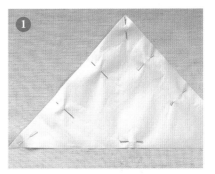

OPTIONS

A tassel makes a great trim for the pointed ends of this runner. Take two tassels and baste one into the point at each end of the main fabric, on the right side. The fringed ends of the tassels should face in toward the center of the fabric. Make up the runner as above.

TAB-TOP CURTAIN

This unlined curtain is very easy to make – most of the effort required is in measuring up before you begin and working out the amount of fabric you will need. The curtain hangs from tabs – loops of fabric that are slipped over a suitable pole. Make sure your pole is fixed far enough above the window to allow room for the tabs.

First, you need to decide what length you want your finished curtain to be and then you can measure up to work out how much fabric you will need. Measure 4½" (12 cm) down from your curtain pole; then measure down from this point to where you want the curtain to end to find the curtain length. Add on 11¼" (28.5 cm) for turnings and facings for the cut length.

Measure the width of your pole and multiply this by one and a half to find the curtain width. If you are making a pair of curtains, divide this by two to find the width of each one. Divide the curtain width by the width of your fabric. Round this up to find how many widths of fabric you need. Multiply this figure by the cut length to work out how much material you will need for the curtains. You will also need extra for the tabs: 12" (30 cm) of 54" (140 cm) wide fabric is enough for eight tabs, so increase the amount of fabric as necessary.

YOU WILL NEED

• Fabric, to calculate the amount you will need, see left

• Basting and matching thread

27 Making up

Before you begin, you may need to join widths of fabric to get the correct curtain width. If you are using plain fabric then simply cut enough pieces to the required length (see page 26) and stitch together, taking ⅝" (1.5 cm) allowances. If you are using a patterned fabric, make sure you cut your lengths to allow for joining the pattern. This also applies if you are making two curtains, as you will want the pattern to line up when the curtains are hung.

You also will need to cut a backing panel for each curtain you are making; this should be the same width as the curtain by 4¼" (11 cm) high. Again, you may need to join widths of fabric.

Each finished tab is 3" (7.5 cm) wide; work out how many tabs you can fit across your curtain width, allowing for 6–9" (15–23 cm) between each one. You will need to cut this many pieces of tab fabric, each one 6¾ x 10¾" (17 x 27 cm). The instructions below are for making one curtain, you simply repeat the method, where appropriate, for two or more.

1 Fold each tab in half lengthwise, right sides together, and stitch the long edges together, taking ⅜" (1 cm) allowance. Press each seam open then turn each tab to the right side. Press each one so the seam is centered on one side of the tab.

SEW SMART
Tab-top curtains work well in sheer fabrics but you must take care to make your seams and turnings as neat as possible since they will show through to the right side. Use flat-fell seams (see page 17) and rolled hems (see page 19).

2 Turn under ⅜" (1 cm) on both side edges of each curtain piece; press. Turn under the sides again by ⅝" (1.5 cm); press. Topstitch along each side. Turn under 3¼" (8 cm) along the bottom edges; press. Turn under the hem by the same amount again; press. Topstitch the hem in place.

3 Fold each tab in half widthwise, wrong sides together. Pin a tab to each top corner of the curtain, matching raw edges and making sure the outer edges of the tabs line up with the sides of the curtain. Baste in place. Pin the remaining tabs across the top of the curtain, matching raw edges and spacing them evenly across the width; baste.

4 Pin the backing panel to the top of the curtain, right sides together, so the curtain is centered on the panel. Stitch across the top of the curtain, taking a ⅝" (1.5 cm) allowance. Fold the backing over to the wrong side of the curtain; press.

5 Turn under the sides of the backing so they match up with the sides of the curtain; press. Turn under the bottom of the backing by ⅝" (1.5 cm); press. Pin to the curtain then topstitch around all the edges of the backing panel where it attaches to the curtain.

TABLECLOTHS

A cloth can protect your table top from daily wear or camouflage existing defects but it's also a quick way of adding color and pattern to a room or outdoor setting. Square or rectangular cloths are the easiest to make; a circular cloth takes a bit more time and effort.

Unless you're making a cloth for a small table, you will probably have to join widths to get the right amount of fabric. You will want to avoid a seam running across the table's center and this won't be a problem if you are joining an odd number of widths. However, if you are joining an even number, you will have to cut one of the lengths in half lengthwise and stitch one half to each side of the rest of your fabric.

For an everyday tablecloth, choose a washable mediumweight fabric. But sheerer fabrics can be layered over darker materials for more decorative effects. Just ensure your fabric falls well as it drapes over the table.

To decide how much material to buy, measure the table's diameter and the length of the drop you would like. Multiply the drop by two and add this to the diameter plus a further 1¼" (3 cm) for the hem to get measurement **A**. Work out how many times your fabric's width goes into **A** (round up if this is not a whole number).

YOU WILL NEED

• Fabric, to calculate the amount you need, see left

• Basting and matching thread

• Paper and pencil

• Thumbtack and string

• Cutting mat

1 Divide measurement **A** (see page 28) by two to get measurement **B**. Cut out a square of paper to this size. Place the paper on a cutting mat and push a thumbtack into your paper at one corner. Tie a length of string to the pin and tie a pencil at the other end so the string measures **B**, when pulled tight. Keep the string taut and use the pencil to draw a quarter circle on the paper. Cut this out.

2 Cut the material into the required number of lengths. Join the pieces of fabric together using a ⅝" (1.5 cm) allowance and finish the raw edges with zigzag stitch. If you are joining two pieces of fabric together, cut one in half lengthwise and join one half to each side of the remaining piece. When you've joined the pieces, trim the fabric evenly on both sides to the **A** measurement, if necessary.

3 Press the seams open. Fold the fabric in half then in half again. Pin your pattern to the folded fabric so the straight edges of the paper line up with the folded edges of the fabric. Cut around the curve of the pattern.

4 Neaten the raw edge with zigzag stitch. Then machine stitch all around, ⅝" (1.5 cm) from the edge – this will act as a guide when you are folding the hem.

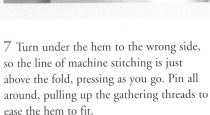

5 Fold the fabric into quarters again. Mark each fold on the fabric edge with a pin.

6 Starting at one pin, work a row of gathering stitches around the edge, between the zigzag and machine stitching, and ending at the next pin. Work another row of gathering stitches between the next two pins, and so on, until each quarter has gathering stitches around the edge.

7 Turn under the hem to the wrong side, so the line of machine stitching is just above the fold, pressing as you go. Pin all around, pulling up the gathering threads to ease the hem to fit.

8 Using catchstitch (see page 11), stitch all around the hem to secure.

RECTANGULAR OR SQUARE TABLECLOTH

Decide on the drop of your cloth, multiply by two, then add 2¼" (6 cm) to get measurement **A**. Add **A** to the width of your cloth to get measurement **B** and to the length to get measurement **C**. Work out how many widths of your fabric go into **B** and round this up if it is not a whole number. Multiply **C** by this number to get the length of fabric you need. Join lengths of fabric to make up a piece that is **B** by **C**. Turn under ⅜" (1 cm), then ¾" (2 cm) all around, mitering the corners (see page 32). Slipstitch the fabric at the miters. Machine or topstitch all around the hem.

BOLSTER CUSHION

aIdeal for brightening up your living room or bedroom, place a sausage-shaped pillow at each end of your sofa or pile them up across the head of your bed. You can use small bolsters to prop up or add interest to a pile of square cushions or pillows. If you plan to use the bolster on a bed, choose white or pastel shades of cotton or satin.

YOU WILL NEED

- Fabric – for amount see below

- Bolster form

- Basting and matching thread

- Ribbon or cord – about 1¼ yards (1¼ m) for the ribbon-tied cover

- Shirring elastic – about 1 yard (1 m) for the elastic cover

- Threader or safety pin for the elastic cover

Making the bolster

Ribbon-tied ends

1 Measure the length and diameter of your bolster form and then add on 32¼" (82 cm) to give you the length of your fabric. Measure the circumference of your bolster form, adding on 1¼" (3 cm) for turnings, to get the width. Cut out a rectangle of fabric to these measurements.

2 Fold your fabric in half lengthwise, right sides facing, and pin along the long edges. Stitch ⅝" (1.5 cm) in from the edge. Press the seam open.

3 Turn under a ½" (1 cm) hem at both ends and press. Turn under an 8" (20 cm) hem and press again. Pin and slipstitch all around the hem. Turn the cover to the right side and insert the bolster form. Tie the ends closed with ribbon.

Elastic ends

1 Measure the length and diameter of your bolster; add these together then add on 2¼" (6 cm). Fold your fabric in half lengthwise, right sides facing, so the long sides match. Pin and stitch the seam, starting 1¼" (3 cm) in and finishing 1¼" (3 cm) before the end. Press the seam open.

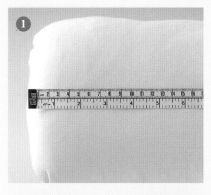

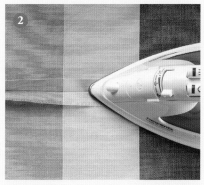

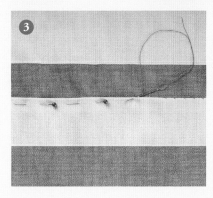

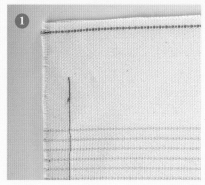

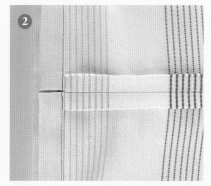

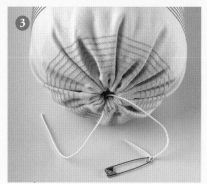

2 Turn fabric under ⅜" (1 cm) then ¾" (2 cm) at both ends of the cover and press. Topstitch around the hems, to make the casings for the elastic. Turn the cover to the right side.

3 Slip the bolster form into the cover. Using a threader or safety pin, thread elastic through the casing at both ends. Use the elastic to pull the openings shut. Tie the ends of the elastic together tightly and trim. Work the elastic around inside the casing to hide the ends.

VARIATION

For a more decorative touch, you can thread cord rather than elastic through the casing and secure with a decorative bow. To clean the cover, untie the bow and ease open the cord (or elastic) to remove the bolster form.

Plain square and rectangular items such as tablecloths, napkins, and placemats, look best when they have mitered corners. Mitering the corners eliminates any bulky or untidy edges and creates a neat flat finish. Mitered corners can be a decorative feature in themselves if they appear on the surface of the item as a border.

The secret to making neat miters is accuracy. For the best results, when you turn under your hems, make sure the depth of each turning is the same all around. These turnings will then be pressed to make sharp fold lines that act as guides for stitching. If your turnings aren't consistent, these fold

lines will not line up correctly. You can make a single or double mitered hem.

For the purposes of this illustration, each turning is ¾" (2 cm) deep, but you can use this technique for any depth of hem. Where it is not possible to have the same depth all around, refer to the box, below.

SEW SMART

Occasionally you may want to make a mitered corner where the side seams are thinner than your hem – say with curtains. In this case, both the side and bottom hems need to be double. Fold your side and bottom hems under once and press. Mark the side hems with a pin at the depth of your bottom hem then fold over the side hems from this point and press in place. Then turn the remainder of the side hem allowances to the wrong side. Pin and press firmly in place to provide a steep diagonal edge at each corner at the bottom. Finally, fold over the other half of the bottom hem, aligning the two diagonal edges of each mitered corner. Pin, press then slipstitch the joins in place and then the side and bottom hems.

Double miter

Use a double miter when you want the miters to appear on the surface of your make, as on the mats pictured above. For the sake of simplicity, the instructions show just one corner being mitered, though you are most likely to be working on four corners at the same time.

1 Turn under ¾" (2 cm) all around and press firmly to make a sharp crease. Turn under a further ¾" (2 cm) and press again. Unfold the hem completely. Fold in a corner so that the folds line up as shown in the picture.

2 Turn under the first hem again all around, and press. Fold back the top edge of the corner so that the point touches the outer folded edge of the fabric; press.

3 Turn under the second hem again all around so that the edges butt together at the corner and pin to hold in place. Slipstitch the edges together at the corner. Press and then slipstitch the hem in place.

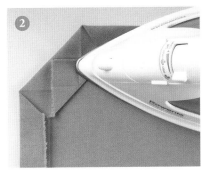

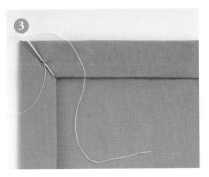

Single miter

Use a single miter when you are going to use a lining, as with curtains. If you are not going to use a lining, then make sure you finish off the edges with pinking shears or a zigzag stitch before using catchstitch. If the hems are not the same size, follow the technique outined in the box, above. These instructions show just one corner being mitered, though you are most likely to be working on four corners at the same time.

1 Turn the hem allowance to the right side all around. Fold the fabric at the corner diagonally from the point formed at the edge of the fabric to the place where the edges of the hem meet; press.

2 Machine stitch along the diagonal fold line. Trim the seam ¼" (6 mm) from the stitching and at the corner, and press the seam open.

3 Turn the hem to the wrong side of the fabric and press. Catchstitch in place all around. If you like, you can pink the edges first.

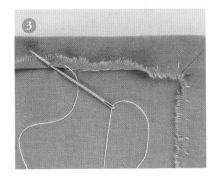

34 Buttons

Most sewing machines will make buttonholes and there are even some that will sew on buttons, too. However, there are times when you'll want to sew a button or buttonhole in place by hand. Buttons that have a loop on their undersides are known as shank buttons; those with holes in them are sew-through buttons. To sew on either type, use special buttonhole thread or your ordinary thread doubled.

When you are making something with a medium- or heavyweight material, the buttons you use need to have a shank to raise them above the overlapping fabric and prevent the button pulling the underlapping fabric. If the buttons you want to use are the sew-through variety, you can create a thread shank when you stitch them in place.

To make machine buttonholes, follow the instructions in your sewing machine manual, making sure you make holes big enough for your chosen buttons.

If you have an older machine that won't do buttonholes, you can make them by hand, although it will take a little longer.

For a machine-made buttonhole, you cut the hole after the stitching is completed; for a handmade one, you cut the slit first. For both types, begin by marking their position on the fabric – draw a line the length you want the hole using an erasable marker. To help you line up buttonholes evenly if you are going to make a row, baste two parallel lines along your fabric, the length of the buttonholes apart.

Sewing on buttons

Stitching a shank button in place

Mark the position of the button. Bring the needle through the fabric at the marked position. Pass the needle through the button's shank and then take it back into the fabric. Bring the needle out again at your starting point. Continue, making five or six small stitches through the shank. Take the needle to the wrong side and fasten off with a few small stitches.

Stitching a sew-through button

1 Mark the position of the button. Bring the needle through the fabric at the marked position. Pass the needle through one of the holes in the button. Lay a matchstick on top of the button and then pass the needle through the second hole and back into the fabric, so the thread passes over the top of the matchstick. Make five or six more stitches in this way, over the matchstick.

2 Take the needle under the button. Remove the matchstick and then lift the button. Wrap the thread around the stitches under the button a few times to form the thread shank. Take the needle through to the wrong side and fasten off with a few stitches.

Four-hole buttons

You can stitch between the holes in a variety of ways. One way is to stitch diagonally across the holes to form stitches that cross. A second way is to stitch between two holes and then stitch between the next two holes to form two parallel lines. A third way is to repeat the second technique between the holes at the top of the lines, to form a square.

Making buttonholes by hand

1 First work a rectangle of small running stitches around the mark, ⅛" (3 mm) from the line on either side and lining up with the ends of the mark. Use matching thread.

2 Cut along the marked line and to make a slit. Using matching thread, oversew the raw edges of the slit with long diagonal stitches. Keep these within the rectangle of running stitches.

3 Work around the slit, inserting the needle just outside the rectangle of running stitches and bringing it out at the edge of the buttonhole. Loop the thread hanging from the eye of the needle from right to left under the point of the needle and draw the needle upward to knot the thread at the buttonhole edge. At the end of the buttonhole nearest the edge of whatever you are making, work the buttonhole stitches so they fan out.

4 At the other end, work a few evenly spaced long stitches, each one the depth of the whole buttonhole. Then work neat horizontal stitches over these to create the bar at the end of the buttonhole. Take the thread through to the wrong side and fasten off.

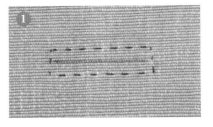

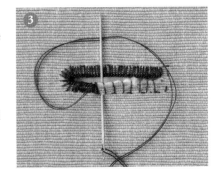

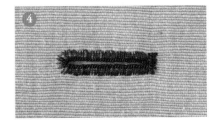

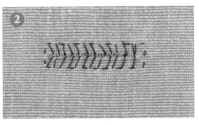

A number of the projects in this book call for fabric fastenings that are ornamental as well as practical. A bias loop is a handmade fabric tube that passes over a button to hold an opening closed. Ties are simple rectangular strips used as trimmings and to secure an item; bias loops also can be used as ties. Tabs are wider fabric strips used to hang curtains or wall hangings from a pole.

Bias loops emerge from a seam and are generally sewn to the edge of fabric before the seam is stitched. If you are making several bias loops, you can make one long tube and then cut it into sections for each loop. Loops should be as long as the combined diameter and depth of the button, plus ¾" (2 cm). Multiply this loop length by the number of loops you need, and cut a bias strip of fabric (see page 52) to this length by 1¼" (3 cm).

Ties also are generally sewn into the seam, so when making them, one short side can be left unfinished. However, if the tie is to be used simply as a trim, then you have to topstitch down all edges. The same is true of tabs.

Purpose-bought fastenings, such as Velcro® and snap tape (see box), can be used for invisible joins.

SEW SMART

If you want to use snaps on an item with a long opening you could use snap tape. This is made up of two lengths of tape with the ball parts of the snaps secured on one side and the socket parts on the other. You simply stitch the tape to either side of the opening, making sure the two parts of the snaps line up exactly.

Making bias loops

Fold your fabric in half lengthwise, right sides together, and stitch between ¼" (5 mm) and ⅜" (1 cm) from the fold, depending on the width of the finished loop. Trim the allowance to ¼" (5 mm). Thread a needle with a doubled length of thread, making sure this is about 2¾" (7 cm) longer than the fabric strip. Secure at one end by taking a few stitches in the allowance. Remove the thread from the needle and then thread it into a bodkin.

Insert the bodkin into the fabric and work it along. As it pulls the thread along the tube, it turns the fabric right side out. Continue until the loop is completely turned through; cut into lengths.

Making ties and tabs

Cut strips of fabric to the required length and width remembering to add on seam allowances on all sides. If the ties are to be sewn into a seam, press in ⅜" (1 cm) on the long edges and one short side. Fold each tie in half lengthwise, wrong sides together. Pin (1). Topstitch along the long edges on each one, close to the edge. Topstitch across the short end (2). If the ties need finishing off, topstitch the other short end.

With tabs, fold in half lengthwise, right sides facing. Stitch both long sides together, taking a ⅜" (1 cm) allowance. Press the seam open so it is centered on the back then stitch across one short end (2). Turn to right side.

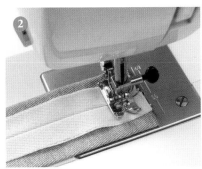

Velcro®

Velcro® is made up of two pieces of tape. One of the pieces is covered with minute stiff hooks, the other with a pile of soft loops. When the two pieces are pressed together, the hooks catch in the loops and hold the tape together. Velcro® can be used for all manner of projects where you want a simple closure for an opening. It comes in different weights, ranging from the soft and lightweight, suitable for delicate fabrics, to the thick and stiff, suitable for heavyweight materials. It can be bought by length and comes in several different widths. You also can buy circles of Velcro® known as coins, which are useful when you would want only a small piece to use as an alternative to snaps. Another Velcro® product has an adhesive backing for sticking to a wall.

Sewing on Velcro®

1 Cut a piece of Velcro® to the length you need and pull the two pieces apart. Mark the positions for the Velcro® on either side of your opening and then pin the pieces in place, turning under the raw ends on each. Pin the hook piece to the underlap and the loop piece to the overlap.

2 Machine or hand stitch around each piece, close to the edge. Stitch diagonally, in both directions, across large pieces of Velcro® for extra security. Remember that your stitching will be seen on the other side, so either sew the Velcro® to a lining or facing, or make a feature of the stitching and combine it with topstitched finishes.

Zippers

Incredibly practical, and because they close an opening completely, zippers work particularly well on anything where you don't want the opening to gape. They are great for a wide range of household accessories and soft furnishings, such as cushion covers and bags.

The instructions on these pages are for the conventional, closed-end type of zipper that is inserted into a seam. This comes in different lengths and weights and has either metal or plastic teeth that are opened and closed with a metal or plastic slider. The teeth are bonded to fabric strips known as tapes. The tapes can be cotton, a cotton blend, or synthetic.

Choose a zipper appropriate for your project. Buy one where the length of the teeth is just slightly shorter than the opening. If you can't get one in the correct size, use a slightly longer one then shorten it (see below). If you can't find an exact color match to your fabric, try to keep to the same shade and just look for one that is lighter in tone. If you are using a patterned material, match the zipper to the background shade rather than any color in the pattern. Make sure the zipper is an appropriate weight – use lightweight zippers with lightweight fabrics, and so on.

SEW SMART
When you are using either of the methods described below and stitching around the zipper on the right side of the fabric, you can use a length of masking tape as a guide. On a centered zipper, use tape that's slightly wider than the slider section and cut a piece that's slightly longer than the zipper. Stick it over the basted part of the seam on the right side and stitch around the edge of the tape when you do the final stitching. On the lapped zipper, use tape that's as wide as the slider and stick it along the basted seam.

Sewing in a zipper

With a centered zipper, the zipper is placed just under the point where the edges of the opening meet. The stitching around the zipper that secures it is visible on the right side. On a lapped zipper, one of the edges of the opening overlaps the zipper and conceals it. The stitching is only visible on one side of the zipper.

Centered zipper

1 Put your two pieces of fabric right sides together and pin along your seam. Mark the beginning and ending of the opening and machine stitch the seam on either side of the marks. Baste across the opening using small, even stitches. Press the seam open.

2 Pin the closed zipper along the seam on the wrong side, right side down, and baste in place. Fit your sewing machine with a zipper foot (see page 15).

3 Stitch around the zipper on the right side, as close to the zipper as possible. Use an unpicker and remove the basting. Open the zipper; when you finish the project and turn the item to the right side, you will be able to turn it through the zipper opening.

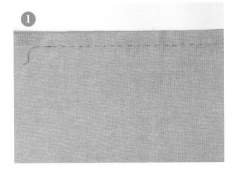

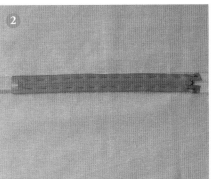

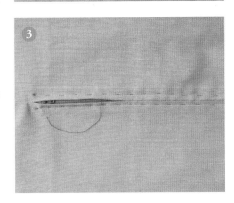

Lapped zipper

1 Prepare your two pieces of fabric as in step 1 of the centered zip. Lay them out wrong side up so the two pieces of fabric are together and one seam allowance extends above the fabric. Place the closed zipper right side down along the seam and pin to the top allowance only. Using a zipper foot, machine stitch in place, close to the teeth.

2 Lay the fabric out flat again and pin the other side of the zipper to the other allowance, pinning through the tape, the allowance, and the fabric underneath; baste.

3 Turn to the right side and machine stitch around this side of the zipper, where the basting is visible, close to the zipper's teeth. Unpick all the basting and open the zipper.

SHORTENING A ZIPPER

Close the zipper and measure the desired length from the top of the slider. Mark this by a pin, inserted in the zipper tape. Set the sewing machine to a wide zigzag but with the length at zero. Stitch across the teeth at the marked point and then trim off the excess zipper below the stitching.

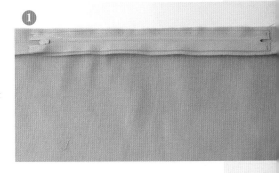

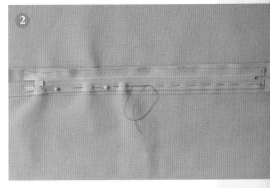

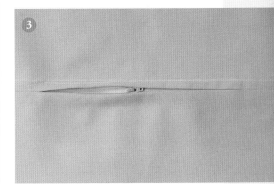

DUVET COVER

It can be hard to find a duvet cover that goes with your bedroom's decorative scheme, so making a custom cover may well be the answer. This cover is made with an overlapping opening that has both practical and decorative purposes – and, using the same instructions scaled down, you can make a matching pillowcase.

By choosing a different fabric for the overlap, you can add a new design element to the cover. The opening is used to insert the duvet and here, a feature is made of the buttons that hold the overlap closed. There are many ways to adapt this design, mostly by mixing and matching different fabrics. You can also add interest with your choice of buttons – there is a wide range of different styles to chose from, or you could cover some buttons in a matching or contrasting fabric.

You will need to use a lightweight material, such as a cotton or poly-cotton mix. Avoid fabrics that are too fine or translucent or you might be able to see the duvet through the cover. French seams are used (see page 17), so that there are no raw edges inside the cover that might become frayed.

YOU WILL NEED

- Main fabric – for amount see below

- Contrasting fabric – for amount see below

- Buttons

- Matching thread

41   Making up

Measure the width of the duvet and add on 1½" (4 cm) for allowances; this is measurement **A**. Decide on how deep you want the overlap and add on 3½" (9 cm) for turnings and allowances; this is measurement **B**. Measure the length of the duvet; this is **C**. Then take away the depth of the overlap, and add 4" (10 cm) for allowances and underlap to this to get **D**.

Cut out one piece of main fabric **A** by **C**, for the back of the duvet cover. Cut one piece of main fabric **A** by **D**, for the lower front. Cut out one piece of contrasting fabric, **A** by **B**, for the overlap section.

1 Take the lower front fabric and turn under ¼" (5 mm), then ⅝" (1.5 cm) along one A-measurement edge. Pin and stitch, then press and set aside. Take the overlap section and turn under ⅜" (1 cm) then 2¼" (6 cm) along one A-measurement edge. Pin, stitch, press.

2 Mark the positions of the buttonholes along the hemmed edge of the overlap section. Make hand or machine buttonholes at these points (see page 35), making sure they are big enough for your chosen buttons. The buttonholes can be made so that they run parallel to the hem edge or parallel to the sides.

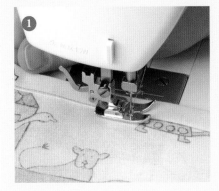

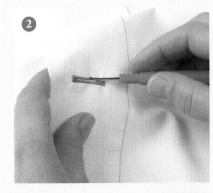

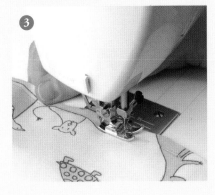

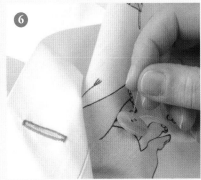

3 Put the two pieces of main fabric wrong sides together, matching the raw short edge on the lower front with a short edge on the back fabric. Pin and then stitch around the raw edges of the lower front, taking ⅜" (1 cm) allowances.

4 Pin the overlap section at the top of the duvet cover, wrong sides together, so that the long raw edge of the overlap section fabric matches the remaining short raw edge of the back fabric. The buttonhole edge should overlap the hemmed edge of the lower front. Stitch around the raw edges of the overlap section, taking ⅜" (1 cm) allowances.

5 Snip across the corners to reduce bulk, and trim the seam allowances to ¼" (5 mm). Turn the duvet cover to the wrong side and press the seams. Pin all around and then stitch, taking ⅜" (1 cm) allowances, making sure you enclose the raw edges to make a French seam (see page 17).

6 Turn the duvet cover to the right side and press. Mark the positions of the buttons on the underlap and then stitch in place (see page 35).

This fabric-covered cube will come in handy as an extra seat or comfy footstool — it can even double as an occasional table. Choose a durable fabric in a shade to match your curtains or other cushions if you want it to blend it with your décor, or chose a differently colored or patterned fabric to introduce new color into your room.

YOU WILL NEED

You can make the cube all in one fabric — try a fake suede for a contemporary look — or clothe each side in a different fabric. Choose different patterns in a subtle range of natural hues or different shades of a single color.

- Fabric — for amount see below

- Foam cube
  The cover has a zipper so it can be easily removed for washing. Because you need quite a long one, you will have to buy the type of zipper that is sold by length — this should be three times the length of one side of the cube.

- Zipper

- Basting and matching thread
  To be effective, each side of the cube should be 18–24" (45–60 cm).

- Zipper foot

43 Making up

Measure one side of the cube and add on 1¼" (3 cm) for allowances. Cut out six squares of fabric to this size.

1 Pin two squares right sides together. Stitch, taking ⅝" (1.5 cm) allowances and beginning and finishing ⅝" (1.5 cm) from the ends. Repeat with two more squares and then join these to the first two in the same way, so you have a continuous loop of fabric that forms the sides of the cushion. Press all the seams open.

2 Pin one of the remaining squares to the bottom of one side square, right sides together. Continue to pin along the adjacent edges for 1" (2.5 cm); baste where you have pinned. Stitch around the basted seam, taking a ⅝" (1.5 cm) allowance. Turn under the same allowance around the base of the cushion sides and press.

3 Turn under ⅝" (1.5 cm) around the remaining raw edges on the bottom square and press. Open the seam out and then lay out the cushion cover so that the bottom square is right side up.

4 Open the zipper and turn it so it is face down. Pin the right-hand side along the opened-out seam allowance, on the right side of the fabric and matching the zipper

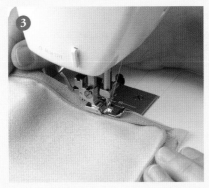

teeth to the pressed line. Snip into the zipper tape at the corners to fit. Stitch along the zipper, close to the teeth, using a zipper foot. Turn the allowance back under.

5 Unfold the turning around the base of the cushion sides and pin and stitch the other half of the zipper to the allowance in the same way. Close the zipper to check the fit and then open it again.

6 Make sure the cover is turned to the wrong side and then pin the remaining square to the top of the cover, right sides together. Stitch, taking a ⅝" (1.5 cm) allowance. Turn the cover to the right side through the zipper. Insert the foam cube and then close the zipper.

SEW SMART

You will probably find that you need to order a cube in your dimensions. Some craft stores sell foam and there also are specialist foam manufacturers from whom you can source a cube. The internet is a good source of information.

ROLL-UP SHADE

Perfect for a small window or glass-paneled door, this simple roll-up shade hangs flat against the wall when you want it down, but then is easily rolled up and tied in place when you want to let the light in. The shade hangs from a wooden batten, secured above the window, so you will need to do a bit of basic DIY as part of this project.

Before you begin to make your shade you will need to prepare a batten from which the shade will hang. This is simply screwed to the wall or window frame above the window. You need to decide how far you want the shade to extend on either side – this will be the length of the batten. Mark the position where you want to fix the batten and measure down from this to where you want the shade to end – this will be the finished length of your shade.

Two screws should be enough to secure the batten for a narrow window, but a wider span may require more. The screws need to be long enough to go through the 1" (2.5-cm) width of the batten and into the wall or window frame. The shade is secured to the batten with stick-and-sew Velcro® (see page 37); the adhesive side of the product is applied to the batten after you've fixed it to the wall.

YOU WILL NEED

- Main fabric, cut to your required measurements

- Lining fabric, enough for your required measurements plus extra for the ties

- Fixing batten – 2 x 1" (5 x 2.5 cm) cut to your required length

- Flat batten – 1" (2.5 cm) wide, cut ⅜" (1 cm) shorter than the fixing batten

- Stick-and-sew Velcro® – the same length as the fixing batten

- Suitable screws and tools

Work out the desired length of your shade and add on 1¼" (3 cm) for allowances. Measure the width of your batten and add on 1½" (4 cm) for allowances and a little extra to overlap the batten at the top. Cut out a piece of main fabric to these dimensions. Cut out a piece of lining fabric the same size. For the ties, take the desired length of the shade and double this; add on 1¼" (3 cm) for allowances for the length. The finished ties are 2" (5 cm) wide, so cut the strips 1¼" (3 cm) wider – 3¼" (8 cm). Cut two strips of lining fabric the same size.

1 Fold each tie in half lengthwise, right sides together. Stitch the long edges of each, leaving a 6" (15 cm) gap in the center. Press the seams open, so they are centered. Cut diagonally across each end and then stitch. Turn to the right side and press again; slipstitch the opening closed.

2 Pin the main fabric and lining fabric right sides together. Stitch around the sides and bottom edge, taking a ⅝" (1.5 cm) allowance. Snip across the corners then turn to the right side; press.

3 Turn under the top edge by ⅝" (1.5 cm) and press. Pin the appropriate part of the Velcro® to the top edge, on the lined side, ensuring that you cover the raw edge of the

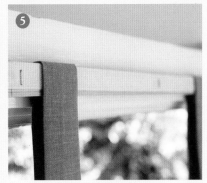

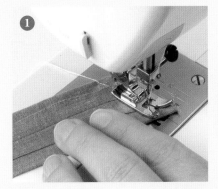

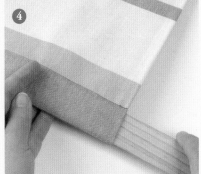

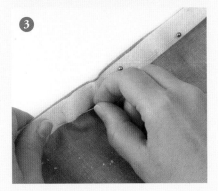

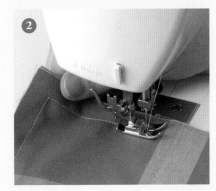

SEW SMART

If you can't get stick-and-sew Velcro® use ordinary Velcro®. Separate it into its two parts. Apply a suitable adhesive to the wrong side of the stiffer part. Press onto the batten. Using a staple gun, staple through the strip at both ends and at intervals along the length.

fabric. Stitch along both sides of the Velcro® close to the edge to secure.

4 Stitch across the bottom of the shade, 1½" (4 cm) above the bottom edge, to make a channel for the flat batten. Unpick the side seam at one end of the channel and then slip the batten in. Slipstitch the unpicked end closed.

5 Fix the 2 x 1" (5 x 2.5 cm) batten above the window in its desired position but don't tighten the screws completely; the batten should stand out a little way from the wall. Slip the ties over the batten so they hang down with the ends level. Tighten the fixing screws. Lift up the ties and apply the adhesive side of the Velcro® to the batten. Press the Velcro® strip on the shade onto the batten. Roll the shade up and knot the ties to hold.

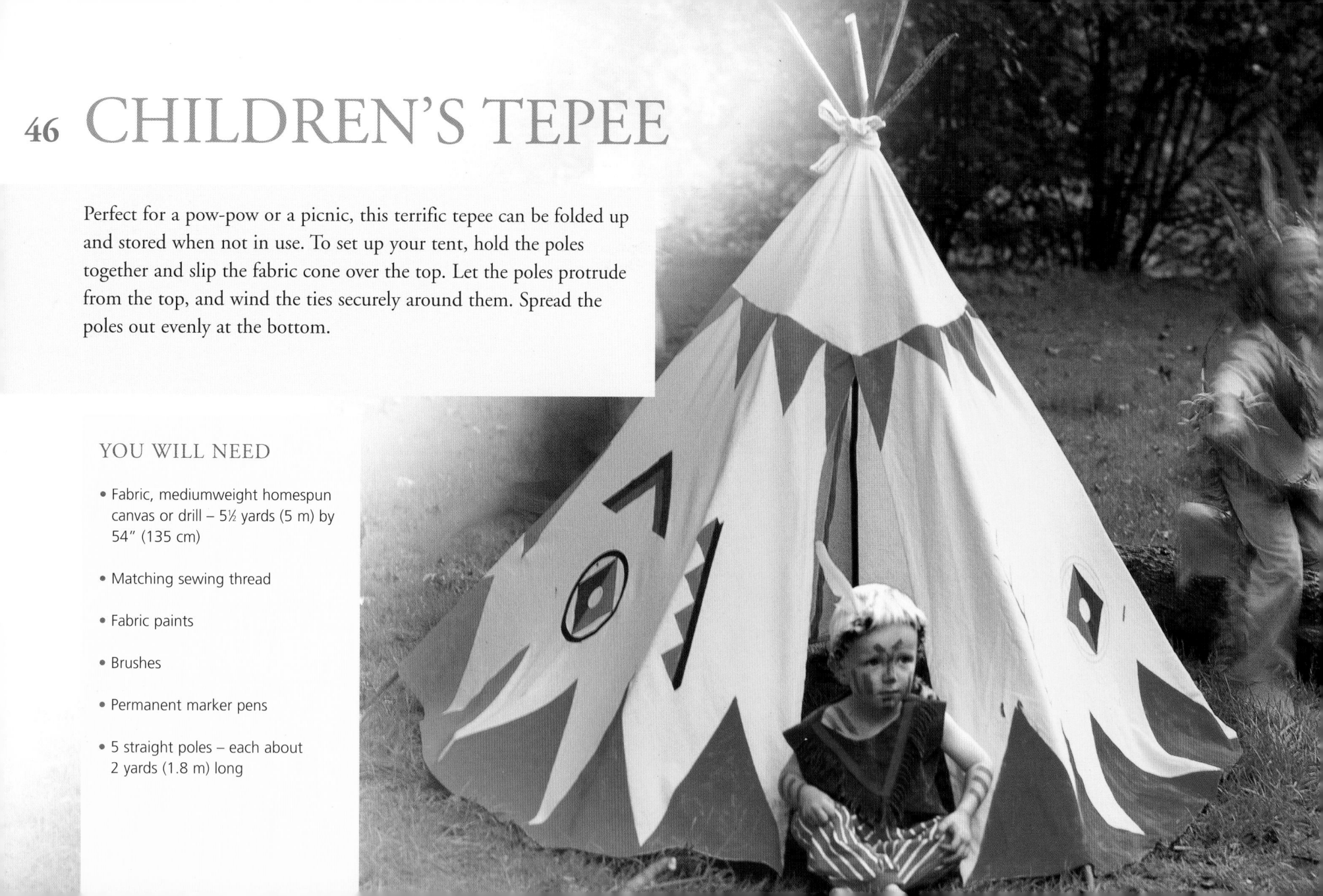

CHILDREN'S TEPEE

Perfect for a pow-pow or a picnic, this terrific tepee can be folded up and stored when not in use. To set up your tent, hold the poles together and slip the fabric cone over the top. Let the poles protrude from the top, and wind the ties securely around them. Spread the poles out evenly at the bottom.

YOU WILL NEED

- Fabric, mediumweight homespun canvas or drill – 5½ yards (5 m) by 54" (135 cm)

- Matching sewing thread

- Fabric paints

- Brushes

- Permanent marker pens

- 5 straight poles – each about 2 yards (1.8 m) long

1 Fold the fabric in half with selvages together and lay out flat. Mark out the pattern pieces according to the diagram.

2 Cut out the pieces, snipping a little off the tops of the **As**. Cut two strips, 4 x 30" (10 x 76 cm), for ties. Reserve remaining fabric for a storage bag (see below).

3 Make the ties (see page 37). Turn under the curved edges of the **A** sections by ⅝" (1.5 cm) and pin, snipping into the fabric as you go. Machine stitch in place. Pin the two pieces right sides together, inserting the ties in one seam, 1¼" (4 cm) from the top.

Stitch, taking ⅝" (1.5 cm) allowances. Turn to right side and press.

4 Finish the raw edges of the two **B** sections with zigzag stitch. Put the right sides together and pin along one straight seam. Stitch, taking a ⅝" (1.5 cm) allowance; press the seam open. Turn under the bottom curved edge by ⅝" (1.5 cm) and pin, snipping into the fabric, then stitch. Turn under the remaining straight edges by ⅝" (1.5 cm); press and stitch in place. Put **A** over **B** so the hemmed edge of **A** overlaps the top zigzagged edge of **B**, making the front edges of the wigwam overlap slightly. Baste the two sections together then topstitch all around.

5 Lay the wigwam flat and mark out your design using a permanent marker.

6 Fill it in using fabric paints. Allow to dry then iron on the wrong side to set the dye, according to the manufacturer's instructions.

A cut 2   (0.20° / 0.5 m)

B cut 2

100" (2.5 m)

54" (1.37 m)

44" (110 cm)

STORAGE BAG
Cut two rectangles 14 x 22" (35 x 55 cm) or join smaller pieces. Place wrong sides together, stitch around three sides, then hem the top, leaving a gap to insert a drawstring cord. Alternatively, follow the instructions for the duffel bag on pages 68-9.

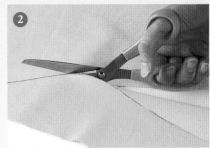
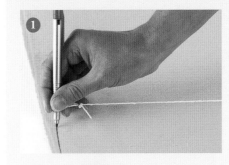

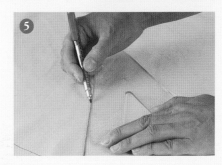

POCKET STORAGE

Most homes are short on storage, so this portable unit can be put to many uses – for socks, panties, or even kids' or kitchen or home office paraphernalia. The organizer is designed to hang from a short curtain pole, fixed to a wall or on the back of a door.

This finished organizer measures 32" (80 cm) long and 26" (65 cm) wide and has three pockets along the top, one in the middle and two at the bottom – snaps hold the pockets shut.

Cut two pieces of main fabric for the front and back of the organizer, each 27 x 33" (68 x 83 cm). Cut the interfacing to the same size. Cut three strips of main fabric for the tabs, each 12 x 5" (30 x 12 cm). For the top pockets, cut a piece of main fabric 37 x 7½" (94 x 18.5 cm) and a piece of contrasting fabric 37 x 3¾" (94 x 9.5 cm). For the middle pockets, cut a piece of main fabric 27½ x 7½" (70 x 18.5 cm) and a piece of contrasting fabric 27½ x 3¾" (70 x 9.5 cm). For the bottom pockets, cut a piece of main fabric 32¼ x 7½" (82 x 18.5 cm) and a piece of contrasting fabric 32¼ x 3¾" (82 x 9.5 cm).

YOU WILL NEED

- Main fabric – 5 feet (1.5 m) of 60" (150 cm) wide fabric

- Contrasting fabric – 20" (50 cm) of 60" (150 cm) wide fabric

- Lightweight fusible interfacing – enough for a piece 27 x 33" (68 x 83 cm)

- Basting and matching thread

- Curtain pole, at least 1 yard (1 m) long

- 9 large sew-on snaps

49 Making up

1 Make tabs (see page 37) and pin one to the top of the front fabric, 1½" (4 cm) in from one corner, matching raw edges and so the right side of the tab faces the right side of the fabric. Pin another tab 1½" (4 cm) in from the opposite corner. Pin the last tab in the center. Baste each tab in place, stitching ⅜" (1 cm) from the raw edges.

2 Iron the interfacing to the wrong side of the back fabric. Pin back and front right sides together and stitch, taking a ⅝" (1.5 cm) allowance and leaving a 12" (30 cm) gap on bottom edge. Snip across the corners then turn right side out. Press, then baste across the gap. Topstitch all around close to the edge, and again, ¼" (5 mm) in from the first row of stitching.

3 Turn under ⅝" (1.5 cm) on the long edge of each strip of contrasting fabric; press. Take the top pocket main fabric and corresponding contrasting fabric and put right sides together so the pressed edge of the contrast fabric is 1¼" (3 cm) below the top edge of the main fabric. Open out the fold and pin the two fabrics together; stitch along the crease. Turn under ⅝" (1.5 cm) on remaining long edge of the contrast fabric; press. Fold the contrast strip over the main fabric; press and pin in place. Stitch along

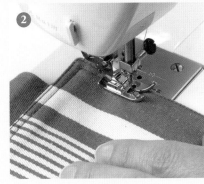

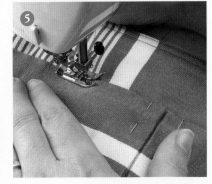

right side of pocket, just below the contrasting strip, to secure. Repeat with the middle and bottom pocket pieces.

4 Turn under ⅝" (1.5 cm) on the raw edges of each pocket piece; press. Pin the sides of the bottom pocket to the tidy, 2" (5 cm) in; topstitch in place. Mark the top of the pocket with pins – one 12" (30 cm) and the other 7" (18 cm) in from the same side of the pocket. Match up the pins and baste the pocket to the organizer at this point; topstitch over the pocket. Fold the fabric into two pockets, each with a folded gusset at either side 2¼" (6 cm) deep; press. Pin then top-stitch across the bottom of the pocket.

5 Pin the top pocket at the top of the organizer 2" (5 cm) in from the sides and top; topstitch in place. Divide the pocket into three equal sections and stitch in place, folding gussets and topstitch as in step 4. Center the middle pocket between the top and bottom pockets and topstitch sides in place. Fold the sides into gussets as before and then topstitch along bottom of pocket.

6 Stitch one half of a sew-on snap inside the center top edge of each pocket and the other half opposite it on the organizer. Stitch one half of a sew-on snap at the end of each tab, on the wrong side and the other half to the corresponding positions on the back of the organizer, just below the tabs.

Bias binding

Bias binding is used instead of a hem to finish the raw edges of fabric. It's made from fabric that has been cut on the bias (see page 7) so is very stretchy and can be eased around shaped edges. It's a neat and sturdy finish and is particularly practical where areas get a lot of use or the fabric is worn or raveled. It's also good for finishing a quilted item to avoid a bulky hem.

You can buy bias binding in limited colors and widths or you can create your own (see pages 52–3). Most commercially produced bias binding is made of cotton but there are also metallic finishes and special, satin binding, which is available to finish off throws and blankets. Ready-made binding is most often sold as long strips that have their edges folded in. (Double bias binding is also available.) You simply place the binding over the edge of your fabric and topstitch once all the way around – which is the fastest method, or machine stitch one side and slipstitch (see page 11) the other side by hand – which makes the stitching invisible. You'll also need to turn the ends of the binding if you are finishing a single edge, and to join the ends if you are binding all around an item.

SEW SMART

Bias binding is often used around the pockets of aprons or tote bags to prevent the fabric tearing at the bottom when fingers push inside or when they are used to hold heavy or sharp objects. For extra security, you can use double bias binding.

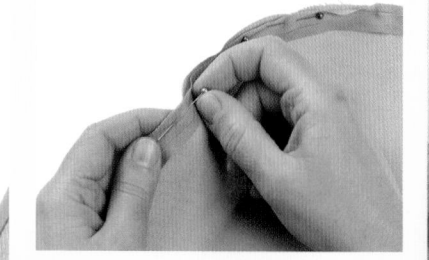

Using bought bias binding

Attaching the binding (slipstitch method)

1 Trim the seam allowance on your fabric to the same depth as the turning on the binding. Open out one turning on the binding and pin it along the edge of the fabric, right sides together and matching the raw edges. Baste and then machine stitch along the fold line.

2 Fold the binding over the fabric edge to the wrong side, so the edge of the binding is just above the machine stitching, and pin in place. Use slipstitch to stitch the folded edge of the binding to the fabric, catching up the fabric in the allowance, just above the machine stitching.

Joining the ends of the binding

Stitch the binding to the edge of the fabric, turning under the raw end at the beginning of the binding by ¼" (5 mm), and when you get to the end, allow the binding to overlap the turned end by about ¾" (2 cm). Fold the binding over the fabric, as before. If you like, slipstitch around the fold of the turned end.

Turning under the ends

1 Stitch the binding to the fabric as in step 1, left. Turn the fabric to the wrong side and trim the excess binding to ⅜" (1 cm).

2 Fold the end of the binding over, so the fold lines up with the edge of the fabric; press. Then fold the rest of the binding to the wrong side as in step 2, left. Use slipstitch to stitch the edge of the binding in place and along the end to secure.

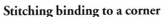

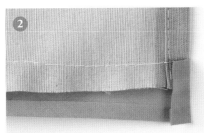

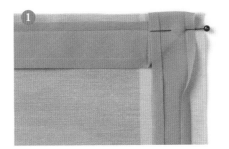

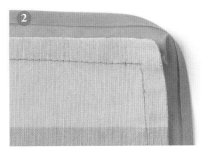

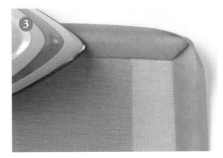

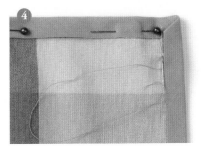

Stitching binding to a corner

1 Stitch the edge of the binding to the first edge of the fabric as in step 1 of attaching the binding, stitching right up to the edge. Fold the binding up to form a diagonal fold at the corner, then fold it down so the edge of the binding lines up with the second edge of the fabric. Pin, baste, then stitch this edge as before.

2 Fold the binding stitched to the first edge up on the right side and then over to the wrong side.

3 Press the binding on the right side into a neat miter at the corner. A diagonal fold will be formed in the binding.

4 Fold the binding over the second edge; you should get a neat miter at the corner on the wrong side. Slipstitch or machine stitch to hold in place.

Home-made bias binding has several advantages — you can make it in any fabric — including the main fabric for your project, and to any width. You can also use it to cover cord and make your own piping (see page 54). A special device, known as a bias tape maker, can make short work of creating your own strips.

Although you can make binding from any fabric, closely woven light- or medium-weight fabrics will give you the best result. Make sure that whatever fabric you use, it has the same care instructions as your original fabric. For a single binding, you need to cut out strips that are four times the desired finished width. You will most likely have to join strips of your fabric together to

get a long-enough length. You'll then need to stitch the binding in place. If you are finishing a single edge, you'll also need to turn the ends of the binding (see page 51) and if you are binding all around an item, you'll have to join the ends. Instructions are given below.

SEW SMART
Using a bias tape maker
This handy device turns both edges of your bias strip simultaneously, making it ready for ironing.
Cut the end of the bias strip on the diagonal and feed it through the tape maker. As the folded strip emerges, press.

Making your own bias binding

Cutting bias strips

If you want only small amounts of binding, you can cut out individual bias strips and join them by pinning two strips right sides together with short diagonal edges matching. Stitch, taking a ¼" (5 mm) allowance. Trim the points at the ends of the seam allowance level with edges of the strip. Or, for a longer, continuous strip, use this method.

1 Take a square or rectangle in your chosen fabric. Straighten the ends and then re-align the grain if necessary (see page 7). Fold the fabric diagonally so the straight crosswise edge is parallel to the selvage or lengthwise-grain edge. Press the fold firmly to create an obvious crease. Unfold the fabric then draw parallel lines on either side of the crease, spaced evenly apart. Trim the fabric to make a square or rectangle.

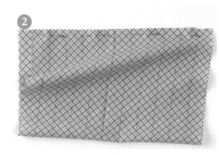

2 Bring the lengthwise-grain edges right sides together, so the cut edge of the fabric lines up with the first drawn line in from the same edge. Pin and then stitch along the seam, just inside the selvage. Press the seam open.

3 Trim off the points at the end of the seam allowance. Begin at one end and start cutting along the marked line. Cut continuously until you reach the end of the marked line.

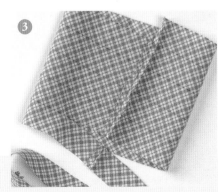

Forming the binding

Use a bias tape maker to turn under the raw edges, then press the folded strip as it emerges. Alternatively, turn under each long edge of the strip by ¼" (5 mm) and press in place.

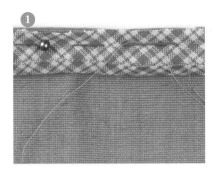

Attaching the binding

1 Trim the seam allowance on your fabric so it is the same depth as the turning on the binding. Open out one turning on the binding and pin it along the edge of the fabric, right sides together. Baste it in place, then machine stitch along the fold line, remembering to turn under the raw end at the beginning by ¼" (5 mm).

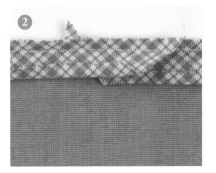

2 When you get to the end, allow the binding to overlap the turned end by about ¾" (2 cm). Cut the end on the diagonal.

3 Fold the binding over the fabric edge to the wrong side, so the edge of the binding is just above the machine stitching, and pin in place. Slipstitch the folded edge of the binding to the fabric, catching up the fabric in the allowance, just above the machine stitching. You can slipstitch around the fold of the turned end, if you like.

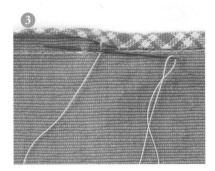

Piping is a popular trimming that's often used on soft furnishings to give seams a firm, definite finish. It is usually of a contrasting color to the main material and is made from a bias strip of fabric that's folded over a length of cord. Piping is sewn between two pieces of fabric so it creates a definite ridge, running along the seam.

Ready-made piping is available in a huge range of colors, fabrics, and sizes but if you want piping to match your fabric, you can make your own (see right). There are several different thicknesses of cord you can buy; you could even use narrow rope if you want a really chunky piping.

Below, you will find information about how to attach piping – you use the same technique whether you are using store-bought or home-made. Whether you are making piping or sewing it on, you need to fit a zipper or piping foot to your sewing machine.

To get the width you need, measure the circumference of your cord and add on 1¼" (3 cm). To get the length, measure along the edge of the fabric on which you want to add the piping and add on 2" (5 cm) for overlaps.

SEW SMART
Making your own piping
Cut a bias strip (see page 53) to your dimensions and your cord to length. Fold the strip over the cord, with right side outermost, bringing the raw edges of the strip together. Pin and baste along the strip, close to the cord. Position the strip under the zipper foot so the needle is up against the cord. Machine stitch along the fabric, keeping the needle close to the cord, but avoiding stitching through the cord itself.

Sewing on piping

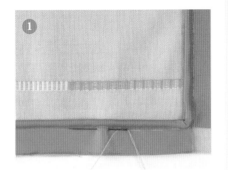

If you are using home-made piping, you can make it to length (see above). If you are buying piping, measure along the edge of the fabric on which you are adding the piping and add on 2" (5 cm) for overlaps.

1 Pin the piping to the edge of the fabric, on the right side, and matching the raw edges of the piping to the raw edge of the fabric. Leave at least ¾" (2 cm) of piping free at the start and finish 1¼" (3 cm) from your starting point. Baste in place. If you're applying piping in a sharp angled corner, snip into the flat part of the piping to ease the fit.

2 Fit a zipper or piping foot and machine stitch around the piping, as close to the cord as possible, leaving the ¾" (2 cm) of piping free at the start. Finish stitching 1¼" (3 cm) from the starting point of your stitching. Take your sewing out of the machine and finish as in joining piping, steps 2 and 3.

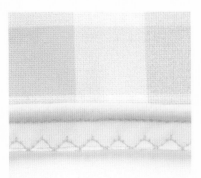

SEW SMART

To ensure a neat finish when sewing on piping, stitch close to the covered cord, following the line of stitching on the piping. When you have finished, use zigzag stitch along the raw edge of the piping and fabric. Alternatively, pink and stitch the raw edges (see page 17).

Joining piping

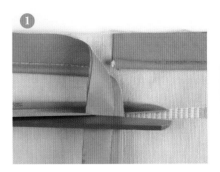

If you are applying a continuous length of piping around an object, you will have to join the ends. If you want to be absolutely certain that your piping won't unravel, you can, if you like, unpick the ends of the old and new cords and interweave them before replacing the bias strips on both ends.

1 When you have finished stitching your piping (1¼" [3cm] from the end), trim it so it overlaps the beginning by ¾" (2 cm). Unpick the stitching in the piping by ¾" (2 cm).

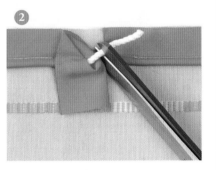

2 Roll back the fabric to reveal the cord. Trim the end so it fits flush with the beginning of the new piping.

3 Turn under ⅜" (1 cm) on the bias strip you just rolled back, then fold this piece of bias strip over the beginning of the piping. Pin in place and then resume machine stitching the piping.

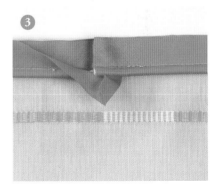

CLOTHESPIN BAG

The clothespin bag has long been a popular household accessory. This one is made to fit over a coathanger, so the bag can be hooked onto the clothesline when you're hanging out the laundry, ensuring the clothespins are close at hand. And, once your things are dry, the bag can be refilled and stored hanging up.

You will need to use a wooden coathanger for this clothespin bag – the shapes of plastic and metal hangers aren't really suitable. The finished size of the bag is approximately 14" (36 cm) high and 16" (41 cm) wide.

Choose a closely woven, light- or mediumweight fabric for this project. The clothespins will weigh the bag down, so a fine fabric or one with too open a weave won't be suitable. Also, the opening on the bag will get plenty of wear and tear when you put your hand in to remove the clothespins.

This version uses contrasting fabric for the left front but it could be made in one fabric only. The same contrasting material has been used to make a matching bias binding that trims the edges and also is used to make a bias tie.

YOU WILL NEED

• Main fabric, 30" (75 cm) of 54" (140 cm) wide fabric

• Contrasting fabric, 20" (50 cm) of 54" (140 cm) wide fabric

• 70" (1.75 m) of 1" (2.5 cm) wide bias binding made from the contrasting fabric (see page 53)

• Basting and matching thread

• Wooden coathanger

• Bodkin

1 Put the fronts and the back right sides together and pin at the "shoulders". Stitch, taking ⅝" (1.5 cm) allowances and press the seams open. Using slipstitch method (see page 51), apply bias binding to the top edge of the right front, across the back then down the top edge of the left front.

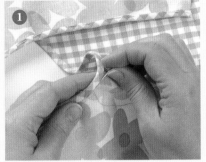

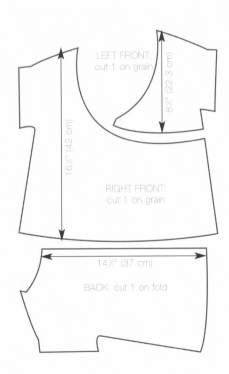

LEFT FRONT: cut 1 on grain

8¾" (22.3 cm)

16½" (42 cm)

RIGHT FRONT: cut 1 on grain

14½" (37 cm)

BACK: cut 1 on fold

USING THE PATTERN

An easy way to enlarge the pattern is to use a photocopier until each piece becomes the same size as indicated on the pattern. You will need to enlarge the pieces three times at 200 percent. You will have to cut out the pieces and enlarge them separately during the enlarging process. When you have finished, trim away any excess paper from your photocopied patterns.

Fold your fabric, place the back pattern so the straight edge is on the fold line and cut out close to the to the paper's edge (the pattern includes an allowance). Then unfold the fabric and cut out the two fronts.

2 Bind the edges of the "sleeves" with bias binding in the same way. Overlap the right front with the left front so the sides line up and pin together. Stitch together, taking a ⅜" (1 cm) allowance, and making sure you don't stitch through the back section.

3 Pin around the sides and bottom and then stitch, taking a ⅝" (1.5 cm) allowance. Snip across the corners and into the curves. Turn right side out and press seams.

4 Topstitch across the openings of the "sleeves" ⅝" (1.5 cm) in from the edge so the hanger fits snugly in the bag.

5 Using a 15" (38 cm) length of bias binding make a bias tie (see page 37). Knot the bias tie in a bow and stitch where the left and right fronts overlap.

APRON

You'll be more than happy to reach for this practical covering when cooking or engaged in other messy tasks. The ruffles add a feminine touch but you have the option of creating a unisex or masculine version by dropping the ruffles and replacing them with bias binding. The pocket, which is shown with center stitching that creates two compartments, can also be attached without the center stitching to make one large pocket.

Choose a light- or mediumweight washable fabric for both the apron and pockets. The dimensions below will suit a person of average size. If you want a larger size, measure from the top of the armhole to just above the knee for length and around the waist for the width. Don't forget to add extra for the ties, neck loop, and pocket.

From the main fabric, cut one piece 28¾ x 30½" (73 x 77 cm) for the body of the apron; two pieces each 2¼ x 25" (6 x 63 cm) for the side ties; one piece 2¼ x 24" (6 x 60 cm) for the neck loop; one piece 2¼ x 19¾" (6 x 50 cm) for the top ruffle, and one piece 2¼ x 45" (6 x 115 cm) for the bottom ruffle. From the contrasting fabric, cut one piece 8¼ x 12½" (21 x 32 cm) for the pocket and one piece 3 x 28¾"(7.5 x 73 cm) for the bottom trim.

YOU WILL NEED

- Main fabric – for amount see left

- Contrast fabric – for amount see left

- Bias binding – for amount see step 2 below

- Basting and matching thread

- Erasable marker

1 Fold the body piece in half lengthwise, right sides together. Mark 7½" (19 cm) in from one corner and on the adjacent long edge 9½" (24 cm) down. Run lines of pins down from the top mark and in from the side mark until they meet. To shape the armholes, cut down one line of pins, but curve off the corner before cutting along the second line of pins. Make sure you cut through both layers of fabric.

2 Take the pocket piece and fold it in half widthwise, right sides together. Place a large plate in one corner where the raw edges meet and draw around the curve. Cut around the drawn line to shape the pocket. To work out how much bias binding you need: measure around the curved edge of the pocket; measure around the shaped armholes and multiply this by two; then add these two measurements to 55½" (140 cm) to get the final amount.

3 Make side ties and neck loop (see page 37). Stitch one end of each tie, leaving all other ends raw.

4 Turn under a double ¼" (5 mm) hem on one long edge of the ruffle; topstitch. Using basting stitches, gather up the other long edge (see page 66). Pin ruffle to apron top, right sides together; baste.

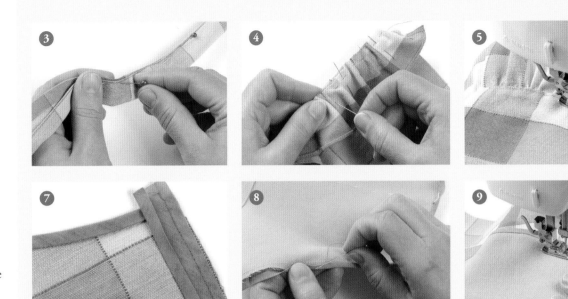

5 Pin one end of the neck loop to the top of the apron, ⅜" (1 cm) in from the edge and on top of the ruffle, matching raw edges. Pin the other end of the loop to the opposite side. Machine stitch across the top of the apron to secure the ruffle and loop. Turn to the right side and press lightly so the ruffle stands up. Topstitch along the top of the apron, through the ruffle fabric.

6 Make and attach the bottom ruffle to the bottom of the apron as above, but without topstitching. Take the strip of contrasting fabric and turn under ⅜" (1 cm) along both long edges; press. Pin the fabric, right side up, along the bottom of the apron so the bottom edge of the trim is lined up with the bottom edge of the apron. Topstitch along the folded edges of the trim to secure.

7 Pin the side ties in place, ⅜" (1 cm) down from the corners, matching raw edges; baste. Using slipstitch method (see page 51), apply bias binding to the armholes, starting at the top of the ruffle. Cut the binding flush with the apron's straight edge and then bind the straight edges, including the edges of the bottom ruffle.

8 Turn under the straight edge of the pocket by ⅜" (1 cm); press. Turn under again by ⅝" (1.5 cm); press and pin. Topstitch along the hem. Fold the pocket in half and mark the fold with basting. Bind the curved edge.

9 Pin the pocket section in the desired position. Topstitch around the edge, just inside the bias binding. Then topstitch along the line of basting to divide the pocket in two.

DIAPER STACKER

This is one baby's accessory that will get a lot of use and it can accommodate both disposable and cloth diapers. It incorporates a child-size plastic or wooden hanger so it's easy to suspend near the changing table. The seams are trimmed with a contrasting piping – you can make your own (see page 54) or buy ready-made in a suitable color.

For this project you need to make two patterns, one for the top section and one for the sides. For the top pattern, place your hanger on the paper and draw around the curve at the top; mark the position of the hook. Draw an 8" (20 cm) line down from the hook. Draw a horizontal line across the bottom of this line, making sure it lies at right angles to the vertical line. Join the ends of the curved line to the horizontal line with straight lines parallel. Cut out the shape.

To make the pattern for the sides, cut out a rectangle of paper 10 x 19" (25 x 48 cm). Fold the paper in half lengthwise and make a pencil mark ¾" (2 cm) from the fold on one short edge. Using a ruler, join this mark to the bottom corner of the paper (not the corner made by the fold). Cut along the line and then unfold the pattern. You should have a long shape with slanted sides, like a triangle with the tip missing.

YOU WILL NEED

- Main fabric, around 1 yard (1 m) of 56" (140 cm) wide fabric

- Lining fabric, about ½ yard (50 cm) of 56" (140 cm) wide fabric

- Firm interfacing, about 10 x 20" (25 x 50 cm)

- Piping – you will need to make or buy about 4⅜ yards (4 m)

- Child's wooden or plastic coathanger

- Paper, pencil, and ruler

- Basting and matching thread

61 Making up

Use your top piece pattern to cut two pieces of fabric, adding on ⅜" (1.5 cm) all around. Measure the width of the bottom of one fabric piece. Cut out a piece of fabric this measurement by 10" (25 cm) for the base section. Cut out one piece this measurement by 19" (48 cm) for the back. Cut another piece of fabric the same length but 1¼" (3 cm) wider and then cut it in half lengthwise to make the two front pieces. Use the side pattern to cut out two pieces of fabric.

Take the base section and cut a piece of lining fabric the same size and a piece of the firm interfacing that is ⅜" (1.5 cm) smaller all around.

Measure around the long edges and one short edge of the back; you will need two lengths of piping this measurement plus a bit extra for turnings. You will also need two 20" (50 cm) lengths for the front openings. Measure the width of one top piece again; you will need a length of piping twice this plus a bit extra.

1 Pin the two top pieces right sides together and stitch around the sides and top taking a ⅜" (1.5 cm) allowance and leaving a small gap for the hook.

2 Apply piping to one long edge on each front piece. Turn under each piped edge and topstitch each hem in place, close to

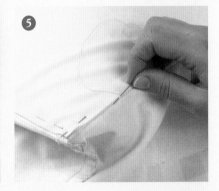

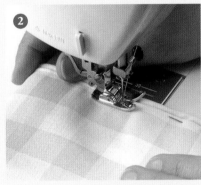

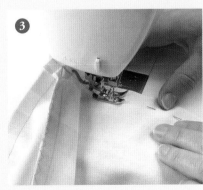

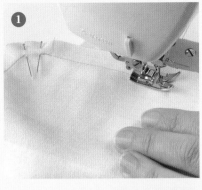

the piping. Apply piping along remaining raw long edge on one front piece and continue it across one short edge, then across one short edge of the other front piece, so the piped hems meet. Continue piping along the remaining raw long edge. Apply piping around two long edges and one short edge of the back piece.

3 Pin the side pieces to the front section, right sides together and stitch the seams, close to the piping, finishing the seam ⅜" (1.5 cm) from the bottom. Repeat to stitch the back to the sides. Pin the main fabric base section to the bottom of the stacker, right sides together and stitch.

4 Put the interfacing into the base so it sits snugly under the seam allowances. Baste all around the interfacing, stitching through it and the allowances to hold in place.

5 Turn under ⅜" (1.5 cm) all around the lining piece; press. Put this into the base so it sits on top of the interfacing. Pin to the allowances then handstitch in place.

6 Apply piping all around the bottom of the top section. Put the main body of the stacker and the top section right sides together. Pin the top edge of the main body to the bottom edge of the top section, matching raw edges and making sure the front opening is centered. Stitch all around, close to the piping and using a zipper foot.

EYELET CURTAINS

An eyelet heading gives curtains a sleek, modern appearance. The eyelets are created by special tape and rings, which are attached along the top of the curtain so that the curtain pole is inserted through the fabric. When you hang your curtain, you need to weave the pole in and out of the eyelets.

For this kind of curtain you need to begin by cutting the right length of eyelet tape. Multiply the length of your curtain pole by one and a half to find the curtain width. If you are making two curtains, halve this to find the width of each one. Cut your curtain tape to this measurement plus 1½" (4 cm). You need the holes in the tape to be evenly spaced so you may need to cut the tape slightly longer – if you do, measure the tape and use this as the curtain width measurement.

Measure from your curtain pole to the point where you want the curtain to end; add on 4" (9.5 cm) to get the curtain length. Add on 6" (15 cm) for turnings to find the cut length. Divide the curtain width by the width of your fabric. Round this up to find how many widths of fabric you need. Multiply this figure by the cut length to work out how much material you will need for the curtains.

YOU WILL NEED

• Main fabric, to calculate the amount you need, see left

• Contrasting fabric, 7½" (19 cm) x the curtain width

• Eyelet tape, to calculate the amount you need, see left

• Matching and basting thread

Making up

As for the tab-top curtain (see page 27), you may need to join widths of fabric to get your curtain width. Cut your lengths of fabric as required and stitch them together.

1 Turn under ⅜"(1 cm) on both side edges; press. Turn under the sides again by the same amount; press. Topstitch each turning in place. Turn under ⅝" (1.5 cm) along the bottom edge; press and then topstitch in place.

2 Pin the border to the curtain top, the right side of the border to the wrong side of the curtain, and so the curtain is centered on the border. Stitch across the top of the curtain taking a ⅝" (1.5 cm) allowance.

3 Fold the border to the right side of the curtain; press. Turn under the sides of the border so they match up with the sides of the curtain; press. Turn under the bottom of the border by ⅝"(1.5 cm); press. Pin the border to the curtain then topstitch all around the border, close to the edges.

4 Position the eyelet tape across the top of the curtain, on the wrong side, so that the tape is positioned just below the topstitching that runs along the top of the border. Following the manufacturer's instructions, pin the tape in place, turning

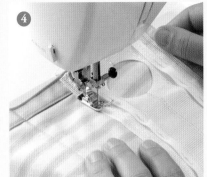
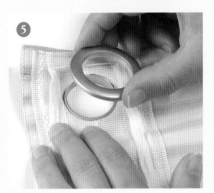
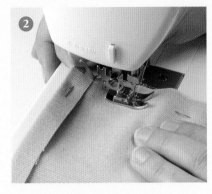

the ends under at the curtain edges. Stitch along the bottom and top of the eyelet tape, making sure you stitch in the same direction along each edge. Stitch over the ends of the tape. Take care not to stitch over the gathering cords.

5 Use a pair of small scissors and cut away the fabric at the eyelet holes, making sure you cut through both layers of fabric. Following the manufacturer's instructions, fix the eyelets over the holes.

6 Hang the curtain on your pole. Tie the gathering cords together at one end. Pull on the other end until the curtain is the width you require; tie the loose ends together and tuck out of sight. Turn up the bottom edge of the curtain until it is the required length; pin. Take the curtain down and hem the bottom edge before re-hanging.

SEW SMART

Eyelet tape is similar to curtain tape but has holes along its length at regular intervals. Cords run along the top and bottom of the tape – these are gathered up when the curtain has been made to draw it into folds. Some tapes also feature colored markers and sewing lines that act as guides when you are stitching. Once the tape has been sewn to the top of the curtain, the fabric you can see behind the holes is cut away and the eyelet rings pressed in place – these cover the raw edges of the fabric. The rings should be removed before the curtains are cleaned, but they are easily levered apart with a small screwdriver.

Appliqué

As the name suggests, appliqué allows you to apply one piece of fabric to another. This simple decorative technique is great for adding charm and a personal touch to your soft furnishings.

Appliqué is a great way to add decorative motifs to your projects. Even simple shapes such as hearts, stars, and cubes, work well but more elaborate animals, initials, and flowers, could be attempted. Cookie cutters can provide the outlines for many shapes.

Use the basic method to stitch your shapes to accessories and soft furnishings. If your shape has many different edges, it is probably easier to use the oversew appliqué method. You can, of course, use more than one shape and build up a picture by using several layers and different elements. It is also possible to combine appliqué with decorative stitching to add detail at the same time as securing the fabric in place.

Another simple way to apply appliqué is to use an iron-on backing (see page 69).

FELT SHAPES

Because it doesn't fray, felt is a good choice for easy appliqué. Use a template to cut out your shape then pin and baste the felt to the main fabric. Stitch around the shape, close to the edge, to secure. A simple running stitch looks very effective, or you could try blanket stitch (see page 11) in a contrasting color. Cutting out the shapes with pinking shears looks good, too.

Basic method

Here, the edges of the appliqué fabric piece are turned under and the patch is stitched to the background fabric. Traditionally, slip stitch is used but running stitch or even machine stitching are also effective as long as you stitch close to the folded edge.

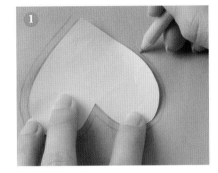

1 Make a paper template and place this on the wrong side of your appliqué fabric; draw around the edge. For the allowance, draw around the shape again, ¼" (5 mm) outside the first line. Remove the template.

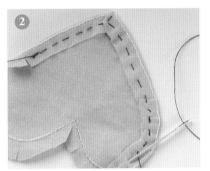

2 Machine stitch just outside the inner marked line. Cut out the shape using the outer line as a guide. Snip into any curves or corners. Turn the allowance under and pin in place, making sure the machine stitching is visible on the turning; baste.

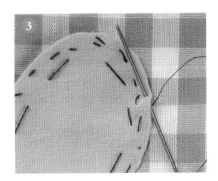

3 Pin and baste the appliqué patch, right side up, to the right side of the main fabric. Stitch around the edges to hold in place. Remove all basting stitches.

Oversew method

With this technique you use a machine or embroidery stitch to oversew the edges of the patch when stitching to the fabric. There is no need, therefore, to turn under the edges of the patch.

1 Draw around your template on the right side of your appliqué fabric. Cut out roughly, leaving an ample allowance around the drawn line. Pin and baste to your main fabric then machine stitch in place, following the drawn line.

2 Using a small pair of sharp scissors, trim away the allowance, close to the machine stitching. Select a zigzag stitch where the stitches will be close together and sew around the shape, covering the raw edges. Alternatively, you can hand stitch all around, using buttonhole stitch (see page 35).

Using trims

Home-sewn projects can be given that special touch that lifts them out of the ordinary by adding a decorative trim. This simple cushion, for example, has been made up with two different fabrics. A plain ribbon is stitched over the seam and a pleated ribbon is stitched at each end of the panel. Circles cut from embroidered fabric make the perfect appliquéd decoration (see page 64).

Trims fall into two types – those that are bonded to a length of tape (the insertion tape) that is concealed inside a seam or under a turning – and flat trims. When you stitch flat trims into a seam or under a turning you conceal part of the decorative element. Therefore, flat trims are ideal for stitching over a hem or seam. Beaded and bobble trims generally come on an insertion tape, and you can also buy ready-made ruffles, where the fabric is gathered onto the insertion tape. Some lace is attached to tape, but generally lace is sold as a flat trim, as is ribbon, braid, and rickrack.

RUFFLES

Cut a fabric strip to at least double the length of the piece to which you will add it and to the desired width, remembering to add seam allowances all around, if appropriate.

Take your strip and hem one long and two short edges as required.

Run a line of basting stitches for gathering along the remaining raw long edge, leaving a loose thread at the beginning and end. Pull on the loose ends of the basting thread to gather the ruffle so that it fits the dimensions of the fabric you are trimming. Pin the pieces together, baste, then stitch.

Adding trimmings

Stitching a trim to a hem

1 Turn under your hem allowance and press in place. Unfold the hem and lay out the fabric flat, right side up. Take your trim and match up the bottom edge of the insertion tape to the fold line; pin along the insertion tape; baste.

2 Turn under your hem again. Press again and pin in place. Hand or machine stitch the hem – the trim will hang below the edge of the hem.

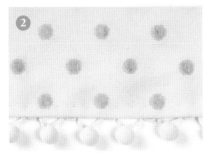

Using a trim as hemming

When adding a decorative trim to the edge of a project, you can use the stitching that secures the trim to hold a hem in place. Begin by turning under your hem and pressing it, then baste along the hem.

Lay your trim over the hem so it covers the basting, turning under the ends of the trim; pin. Stitch over the trim, making sure that you stitch through the hem. Here, rickrack has been stitched using herringbone stitch. Working from left to right, bring the needle and thread to the right side of the fabric at the bottom of the trim. Take the needle and thread across the trim and take a small stitch through the hem at the top of the trim where the curve dips down, inserting the needle from right to left. Repeat to make a stitch at the bottom of the trim. Continue in this way to the end of the trim. Using a thread that matches the trim will conceal the diagonal stitches. Choose a contrasting thread and you can make a feature of the stitching.

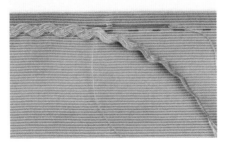

Stitching a trim in a seam

1 If using a flat trim, like rickrack, press under the allowance on one of your pieces of fabric. Unfold, then baste the trim along the allowance on the right side, so that part of the trim is above the pressed fold. Pin your pieces of fabric right sides together and stitch, making sure you take the correct allowance. Press the seam open; the trim will be between the two fabrics.

2 If using a trim with an insertion tape, press under the allowance as above. Unfold and pin the trim along the allowance, on the right side, so that the bottom edge of the insertion tape lines up with the pressed fold; baste in place. Stitch your pieces of fabric together as above; when the seam is pressed open, the trim will be sandwiched between the two fabrics.

Using a trim to cover a seam

Begin by pressing your seam open. Cut your flat trim to length and pin over the seam, turning under the ends of the trim. Secure with basting: If the trim is narrow, make diagonal stitches, zigzagging over the trim; if it is wide, baste along either side. Machine stitch in place along each side of the trim. You also can use a strip of contrasting fabric in the same way. Simply cut to length and turn under the raw edges before basting.

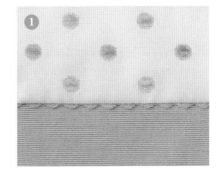

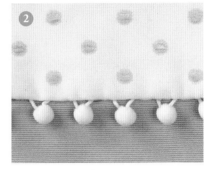

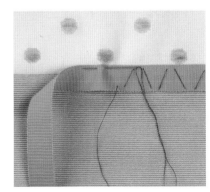

DUFFEL BAG

This simple, roomy bag is the perfect all-arounder. As well as storing toys, it is ideal for a day out at the beach or picnic in the country. The instructions here are for a bag 21" (52.5 cm) high, with a 10" (25 cm) diameter circular base. Make it up in a larger size for a great weekend bag or a storage bag. Choose a hardwearing, mediumweight fabric for the best results.

   This bag is closed by cord threaded through the top hem. For a child-pleasing effect, there's a border of appliquéd animals.

YOU WILL NEED

- Main fabric – for amount see below

- Small amount of contrasting fabric for appliqué (optional)

- Cord, 63" (160 cm) long

- Basting and matching thread

- Threader or safety pin

69 Making up

Cut out an 11¼" (28 cm) diameter circle from the main fabric. Cut out a rectangle of main fabric, 25 x 34¾" (63 x 88 cm).

1 If you are going to use appliqué motifs, lay out the fabric and mark five evenly-spaced positions with lines of basting.

2 Cut out animal shapes from the contrast fabric and apply using the oversew appliqué method (see page 65) or the iron-on method described in the box, right.

3 Fold the fabric in half to bring the shorter edges right sides together; pin. Mark a position along the pinned seam 3⅜" (8.5 cm) from the top. Make another mark 1½" (4 cm) below this mark. Stitch along the seam up to the first mark. Start stitching again at the second mark, then continue to the end of the seam (creating the gap through which to thread the cord). Press the seam open.

4 Turn under ⅝" (1.5 cm) around the top; press. Turn under again 2¾" (7 cm); press and pin. Topstitch around the edge of the hem, ⅜" (1 cm) in from the fold. Topstitch all around again, ¼" (5 mm) from the first line of stitching. Topstitch all around the top of the turning, ⅝" (1.5 cm) in from the pressed edge. Topstitch again, ⅜" (1 cm) in from the pressed edge.

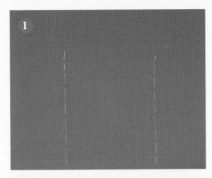
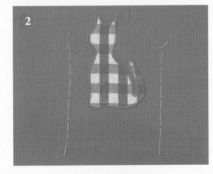

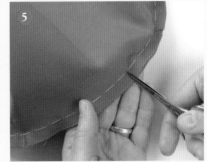

5 Pin the body of the bag and the circular base right sides together. Baste around the edge, snipping into the straight edge of the bag to fit. Machine stitch all around, taking a ⅝" (1.5 cm) allowance. Neaten the raw edges with zigzag stitch and turn the bag to the right side.

6 Using a threader or large safety pin, thread the cord through the casing. Knot the two ends together.

SEW SMART

Iron-on adhesive (sometimes known as Bonda-web) is a useful way to fix appliqué shapes to your main fabric. Draw your shape onto the paper backing. Cut roughly around the shape and then place, paper-side up onto your appliqué fabric. Iron over the adhesive, following manufacturer's instructions. Allow to cool, then cut around your drawn line. Peel off the backing paper and position the shape, adhesive-side down, on the main fabric. Iron to fix then oversew the edges of the shape (see page 65).

CAFE CURTAIN

A café curtain, since it covers only half a window, is ideal when you want some privacy but also light. It is perfect for a small window in a bathroom or hallway. You will need a simple curtain pole that spans the width of your window. Determine the height of your curtain then fix the pole's brackets on either side of your window.

Ideally, fix the pole before you begin the curtain to make it easier to take the required measurements. You need to know the width of the pole between its two supporting brackets; this is multiplied to get the width of the curtain. Here, that measurement has been multiplied by two. However, if you would prefer a curtain that is less full, multiply that measurement by one and a half.

This curtain has been made in a closely woven fabric and trimmed with contrasting material and matching rickrack. As café curtains are generally quite small and with a relatively short drop, don't use a heavy-weight fabric; it won't hang as well as a light- or mediumweight one. You can, however, adapt the style for a full-length curtain – hang your pole above the window and then measure down to the ground or to below the window sill to get your drop.

YOU WILL NEED

• Main fabric, cut to your required measurements

• Contrasting fabric, enough to make two strips as long as your curtain by 1½" (4 cm) and one strip as wide as your curtain by 1½" (4 cm)

• Rickrack in two colors. You need twice the length of your curtain plus the width, plus extra for turnings, in both colors

• Matching and basting threads

• Curtain pole

71 Making up

Measure the width of your curtain pole and double this. Decide where you want the curtain to end and measure from your pole to this point; add on 7" (18 cm). Cut out a piece of fabric to these dimensions.

For the trims: measure the width of your curtain and add on ¾" (2 cm). Cut one strip of contrasting fabric this long by 1¾" (4.5 cm). Cut a piece of white and a piece of blue rickrack the same length. Set all of these aside for the widthwise decoration. Measure the length of your curtain and add on ¾" (2 cm). Cut two strips of contrasting fabric this long by 1¾" (4.5 cm). Cut two pieces of white and two pieces of blue rickrack the same length. Set all these aside for the lengthwise decoration.

1 Turn under ⅜" (1 cm) on both side edges; press. Turn under another ⅜" (1 cm) on the same edges and press again. Topstitch each hem in place. Turn under ⅜" (1 cm) along the top edge; press. Turn under another 2¼" (6 cm) along the same edge and press again. Topstitch the hem in place.

2 Topstitch across the hem 1¼" (3 cm) above the first line of stitching to form a casing for the curtain pole.

3 Turn under 1½" (4 cm) along the bottom edge; press. Turn under another 1½" (4 cm)

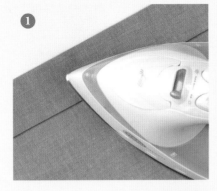

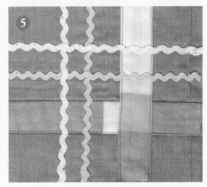

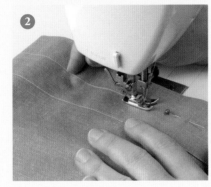

along the same edge and press again. Topstitch the hem in place.

4 Take your lengthwise strips of contrasting fabric and turn under ⅜" (1 cm) on all the raw edges; press. Pin one strip on the right side of the curtain, 1¼" (3 cm) in from the lefthand-side, making sure the strip is parallel to the edge. Topstitch all around the contrasting strip, close to the edge.

5 Pin the widthwise piece of blue rickrack to the curtain, ¾" (2 cm) above the widthwise strip of contrasting fabric, turning under the raw ends neatly. Hand or

Repeat with the second lengthwise strip to stitch it to the righthand-side of the curtain. Repeat with the widthwise strip, stitching it 1¼" (3 cm) above the bottom edge so it covers the hemming stitches.

SEW SMART

This café curtain has been given a ruffled casing at the top. If you would prefer a plainer top edge, add only 4¾" (12 cm) to the desired length of your curtain when you cut out the fabric. Then, at step 2, turn under the top edge by ⅜" (1 cm) first, then by 1¼" (3 cm) before stitching; this turning forms the casing for the curtain.

The easiest way to attach the rickrack to the material is to use zigzag stitch; it also is in keeping with the "movement" of the rickrack.

machine stitch in place. Pin the lengthwise pieces of blue rickrack, about ¾" (2 cm) in from the lengthwise strips of contrasting fabric. Stitch in place. Pin and stitch the widthwise piece of white rickrack ⅝" (1.5 cm) above the blue widthwise rickrack. Pin and stitch the lengthwise pieces of white rickrack ⅝" (1.5 cm) in from the blue lengthwise rickrack.

MINI BEANBAG

This comfy cushion is just the job for children that like to sprawl about on the floor when watching TV. The cushion is filled with polybeads so it takes on the shape of whoever is sitting on it, and supports him or her in complete comfort. If you have a dog or cat, you could make one for your pet.

This charming floor cushion is decorated with appliqué – here, it's sewn on the sides since this is the area that will get less wear but you also could decorate the top and bottom. Simple circles of brightly colored fabric have been used for the appliqué. To repeat this design, take some circular objects in different sizes – such as cups and saucers – and use these as templates when you cut out the patches in step 1.

When you prepare the pieces of fabric for this cushion, you need to cut out a strip for the side panel. If you want to cut this as a long continuous strip then you will need to buy about 2¾ yards (2.5 m) of fabric. You can, however, join two shorter strips of fabric to get the length you require. This means you can buy less material – 1⅝ yards (1.5 m) of 54" (140 cm) wide fabric is enough – since you can cut the strips across the width of the fabric.

YOU WILL NEED

- Main fabric, 2¾ yards (2.5 m) of 54" (140 cm) wide fabric (see left)

- Small pieces of contrasting fabrics, enough to decorate the side of the cushion

- Iron-on adhesive

- Polybead filling – a 3 cubic feet bag

- Matching and basting threads

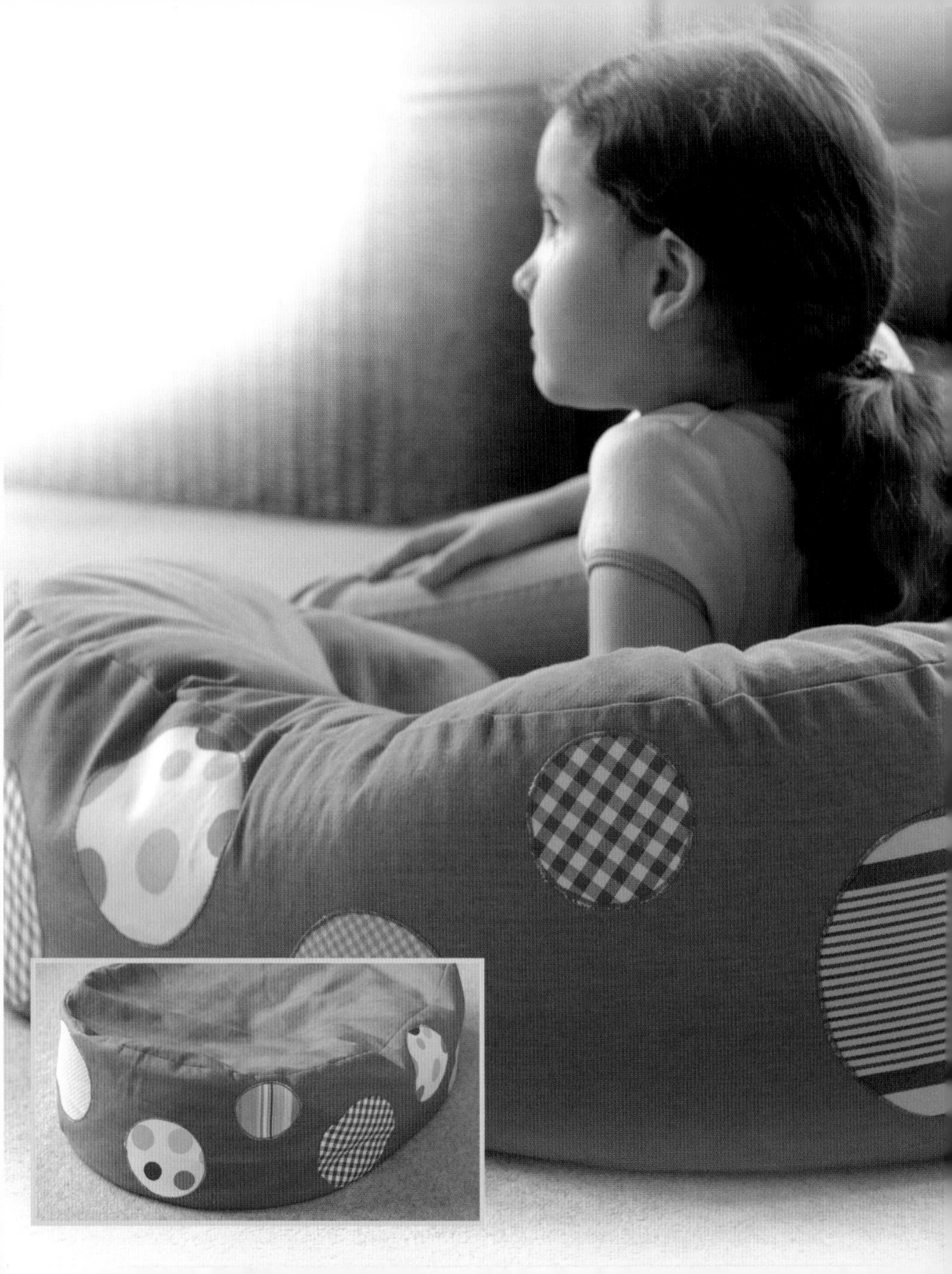

First make a pattern for the top and base of the cushion. Cut out a rectangle of paper 31 x 21" (78 x 53 cm). Round off the corners (see page 21) to make an oval shape. Using the pattern, cut out two pieces of main fabric for the top and base. Measure around the outside edge of the pattern and then cut out a strip of fabric this measurement plus 1¼" (3 cm) by 10¼" (26 cm) for the side.

You will also need a number of different pieces of fabric for the appliqué circles that decorate the side of the cushion. Cut the pieces roughly to size but don't cut into circles yet; this is done after the iron-on adhesive is applied (see step 1).

1 Cut out pieces of iron-on adhesive, each one a bit bigger than the circle you will be cutting out. Iron these onto the wrong side of the contrasting fabrics you are using for decoration (see page 69). Place your chosen circular objects on the paper backing and draw around to make the circles. Cut out each circle.

2 Peel off the paper backing of each circle and iron onto the side fabric, one by one. Set your sewing machine to a narrow zigzag stitch and oversew the edges of each appliqué circle.

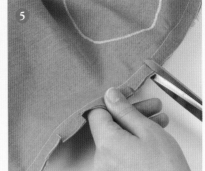

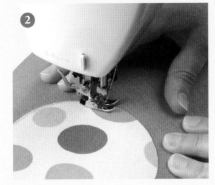

3 Fold the side strip in half widthwise, right sides together and pin along the short edges. Machine stitch along the seam for 1½" (4 cm) at the beginning and at the end of the seam; the gap left in the seam is for adding the filling later.

4 Pin the side strip to the top piece of fabric, centering the seam on one of the longer edges of the oval. Stitch together, taking a ⅝" (1.5 cm) allowance.

5 Snip into the allowance at the curves. Repeat step 4 to stitch the side to the base piece of fabric and snip the curves.

6 Turn the cushion to the right side and pour in the polybeads (see box below). Only put in enough to two-thirds fill the cushion. Slipstitch the gap in the side seam closed using small stitches so the opening is firmly secured.

SEW SMART
Polybeads can be quite tricky to work with – when you handle them, static electricity will cause them to stick to your skin and clothing. The best way to ensure that they get through the gap you've left in the side seam and into the cushion is to construct a funnel apparatus out of paper. Simply take a piece of paper and roll it up into a cone, making sure that there is a large enough hole at the bottom and that your cone fits into the gap in the side seam; secure the paper with sticky tape. To avoid handling the polybeads, scoop them up with a jug and then pour them into the cone.

TOTE BAG

Whether you've got shopping, files, books, or even sports gear to transport, this roomy bag will make sure they reach their destination in style! There's even a handy pocket in which to pop a book, loose change, or your shopping list. Choose your fabric to suit the bag's use; for work or school, a plain, dark material would be better than anything boldly patterned.

A sturdy contrasting fabric has been used for the handles but instead of making up the handles, you could use commercially available webbing. The handles are stitched into the gusset to make them extra strong and are sewn onto the front and back sections before the bag is made up. The simple pocket is made much more decorative by adding an appliqué motif. If you like, choose something to suit the purpose of your bag.

YOU WILL NEED

• Main fabric, 1 yard (1 m)

• Contrasting fabric or webbing

• Basting and matching thread

• Fabric scraps

• Ribbon scraps

75 Making up

Cut out two rectangles 16¼ x 18½" (41 x 47 cm) from the main fabric for the front and back. Cut a 5⅛ x 54" (13 x 135 cm) strip from the main fabric for the gusset. Cut two strips of contrasting fabric, each 4" x 1½ yards (10 cm x 1.2 m), for the straps. Cut a pocket measuring 8 x 10" (20 x 25 cm). You will also need two 8" (20 cm) lengths of ribbon.

1 Stitch one piece of ribbon about 2" (5 cm) up from the bottom edge of the pocket. Cut fabric scraps into shapes for the appliqué and apply to the pocket using iron-on adhesive (see page 69). Zigzag stitch around the shapes for a decorative border.

2 Turn under a double ⅜" (1.5 cm) hem on one short edge of both the front and back pieces. Press and pin. Machine stitch in place close to the edge. Place the pocket centrally on the front of the front fabric piece with bottom edges lined up. Pin and baste in place.

3 Take the straps and fold each one in half lengthwise, right sides together. Stitch, taking a ⅜" (1 cm) allowance, then trim seam and corners. Turn right sides out and press flat, with the seam in the center on one side.

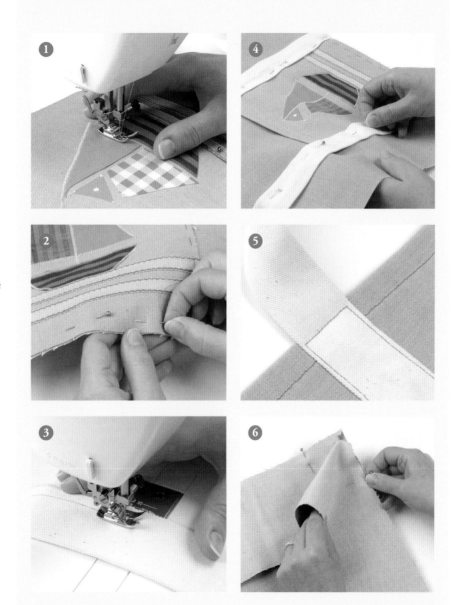

4 Place one strap onto the front of the bag, covering the raw edges of the pocket and with the outer edges 3" (8 cm) from the side edges of the front. The ends of the straps should line up with the bottom edge of the bag. Pin and baste.

5 Topstitch in place beginning at the bottom end. When you get to the top of the bag, continue topstitching across the strap until you reach the opposite edge, then continue down the other side to the bottom. Attach the other strap to the back in the same way, positioning it the same distance from the side edges.

6 Turn under a double ⅜" (1.5 cm) hem on both short edges of the gusset; pin, press, and stitch. Pin one long edge of the gusset around the raw edges of the bag front, right sides together. You will need to snip into the lower corners of the gusset to fit. Stitch taking a ⅜" (1.5 cm) allowance. Repeat to stitch the gusset to the back piece. Finish the raw edges with zigzag stitch. Turn the bag to the right side.

Quilting techniques

Quilting is used to stitch fabric together in layers. It's generally used when you want to sandwich a layer of padding between two pieces of fabric, one of which may be a lining material. This allows you to create something that will keep the warmth in – like a quilt or a coverlet – or to make something that protects against the heat – such as an oven mitt or a placemat. In the past, quilting was generally done by hand but today, it's much faster to use a machine.

Some of quilting's practical elements have developed to become more decorative. The stitching worked to hold the layers together can be used to create intricate patterns.

The simplest quilting designs are formed by parallel lines, either vertical, horizontal, or diagonal, and by crossing lines, to form checks or diamond patterns. However, there are more ornate options. You can buy templates for some of the classic motifs or you can create your own.

If you think you will do a lot of machine quilting, then a walking (or even-feed) foot will be vital. This specialist attachment will feed the layers of fabric through the sewing machine at an even rate, so preventing puckering. With quilting, you usually work from the center out; this helps you to keep the layers smooth.

SEW SMART
When machine stitching a quilting pattern that is made up of parallel lines, a quilting guide is a useful tool. This is fitted to your sewing machine and is set to the distance you want between the quilting. You need only to mark the first line of quilting and stitch along it. For the next, and subsequent lines in the same direction, the quilting guide rides along the previous line of stitching.

Basic quilting

1 Cut out the two pieces of fabric and the padding. Take one of the pieces of fabric and fold it in half diagonally. Use an erasable marker and draw along the fold line. Fold it in half diagonally in the opposite direction and draw along this fold. (This technique will give a diamond pattern – to make checks, fold the fabric in half vertically and horizontally.)

2 Decide on how far apart you want the quilting lines. Draw lines parallel to the fold lines this distance apart, across the fabric in both directions, using an erasable marker and ruler.

3 Sandwich your padding between your fabrics so the right sides of the fabrics are outermost. Pin the layers together, starting at the center and working outward. Working on the backing fabric, so you don't rub out the marked lines as you work, baste the layers together – start from the center, so you baste straight across in both directions and diagonally in both directions. (If you are putting a large piece together, stitch vertical and horizontal lines across the fabric, working from the center out.) Baste around the outside edges.

4 Fit your machine with a walking foot, if you have one, and position the needle in the marked line nearest to the center. Machine stitch along the line to the edge of the fabric. Return the fabric to the sewing machine and insert the needle at the starting point. Stitch along the line in the opposite direction. Pull the loose threads through to the wrong side. Thread them onto a needle and work them into the padding to secure.

PADDINGS

Padding is an essential part of quilting – it's the layer between your two pieces of fabric. You can buy padding, also known as batting, especially for quilting. This is generally a lightweight synthetic material that comes in various thicknesses and qualities.

If you are making an item where you want to add warmth and insulation but not necessarily thickness, then you can use curtain interlining. This is a woven fabric with a soft fleecy pile.

You also could use an old blanket cut to size for your padding. Avoid any worn areas of blanket or the finished item won't be an even thickness. Whatever padding you use, check that the washing instructions are compatible with your covering fabric.

5 Machine stitch along the next parallel line in the same way, then stitch the along the line on the other side of the central line. Continue stitching in this way until you have done all the lines running in the same direction. Then stitch the lines running in the other direction, working out from the center as before.

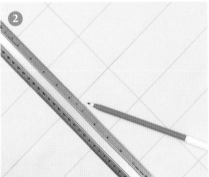

PLACEMATS

Casual or formal, a placemat is a simple way to add interest to a dining or kitchen table. You can create a range of mats in different styles and fabrics to suit any occasion or style of setting. Placemats look effective paired with either a matching or contrasting napkin. These quilted and bias-bound mats are very easy to make. The polka dotted fabric goes well with most décors.

YOU WILL NEED

- Fabric – for amount see below

- Curtain interlining – for amount see below

- Bias binding – for amount see below

- Basting and matching thread

- Erasable marker

- Even-feed foot (see page 15), or quilting needle

Making up

Adding both a decorative touch and more protection for your table, quilting can be done to the entire surface of the mat or just on parts of it. Below, we give instructions for all-over simple quilting. Bias binding (see pages 50–53) as a border produces a hardworking finish and is ideal for rounded shapes.

OPTIONS

There are lots of ways to quilt fabric. The steps below use a simple grid pattern, but more elaborate patterns work well, too. For circular mats, try quilting round concentric lines, working out from the center of the mat. Alternatively, pick a fabric with a printed or embroidered motif on it and quilt around the edge of the design. This technique is known as contour quilting.

1 For each mat, cut out two rectangles of fabric and one rectangle of interlining to your desired finished size. Round off the corners on each piece. (To do this, place a saucer or small plate at the corner and draw around the curved edge. Cut away the fabric, following the drawn line.) Mark your quilting pattern on one piece of fabric. A simple square grid pattern is used here.

2 Sandwich the interlining between your two pieces of fabric so that the right sides of the fabric are outermost. Pin together and then baste, starting from the center and working outward. Trim around the edges to ensure they are even.

3 If using a sewing machine, fit a walking foot, if you have one, and stitch along your quilting lines. If quilting by hand, thread a quilting needle with matching thread and stitch along the guidelines. Remove the basting and erase any marks.

4 Measure all around the edge of the mat and cut the bias binding to this length plus extra for turning. Stitch the binding around the edges to finish, using the slipstitch method and overlapping the ends (see pages 50-53).

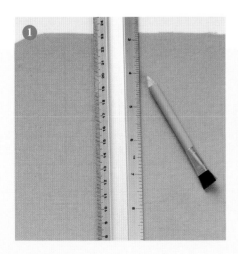

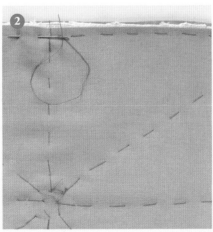

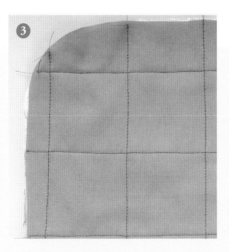

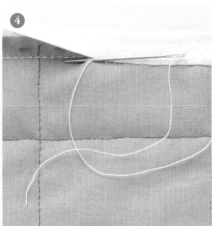

OVEN MITTS

An essential piece of kitchen equipment, oven mitts or potholders are easy to make. Use the same fabric as your tablecloth and other accessories for a coordinated look in your kitchen. These mitts are padded with curtain interlining to give them the necessary thickness that will help protect hands from hot pots and pans.

Traditional quilting techniques are used to hold the layers of fabric and padding together. You can use simple straight lines of quilting or you might like to try for a more decorative effect and quilt in more unusual patterns or use contour quilting to follow the design on your chosen fabric. See page 76 for more quilting ideas and information.

You'll need to use a hardwearing, closely woven fabric, preferably one that's washable. Make sure you pick a washable interlining, too. The oven mitts made here use different but complementary fabrics on the front and back but you can use the same fabric throughout or a lining fabric for the inside of the hand sections.

YOU WILL NEED

• Main fabric – for amount see below

• Contrasting fabric – for amount see below

• Curtain interlining – for amount see below

• Bias binding, 2¾ yards (2.5 m)

• Paper, pencil, and small plate

• Erasable marker

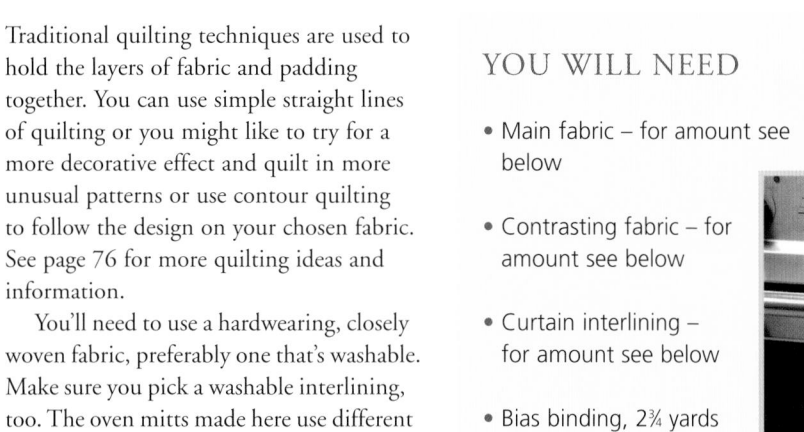

Cut out a piece of paper 7 x 10" (18 x 25 cm). Round off two of the corners on one short side (see page 21). Trim away the paper around the curve. Use the paper pattern to cut out four pieces of main fabric and two pieces of interlining. Cut out one rectangle of main fabric 7 x 31½" (18 x 80 cm). Cut a piece of contrasting fabric and piece of interlining the same size. Use the pattern as a guide to round off the corners on both rectangles of fabric and the interlining. Cut one 4¾" (12 cm) and two 7" (18 cm) lengths of bias binding. Cut one 77¼" (196 cm) length of binding.

1 Take one of the long pieces of fabric and, using an erasable marker, mark the desired quilting lines on the right side. Do the same on two of the smaller pieces of fabric. Take the two long pieces of fabric and the interlining and sandwich the interlining between the fabric so the right sides of the fabric are outermost; pin. Repeat with the smaller pieces. Baste the pieces together, working from the center outward.

2 Stitch along the marked lines on the longer piece. Baste the smaller pieces of fabric and interlining together and then stitch along the quilting lines.

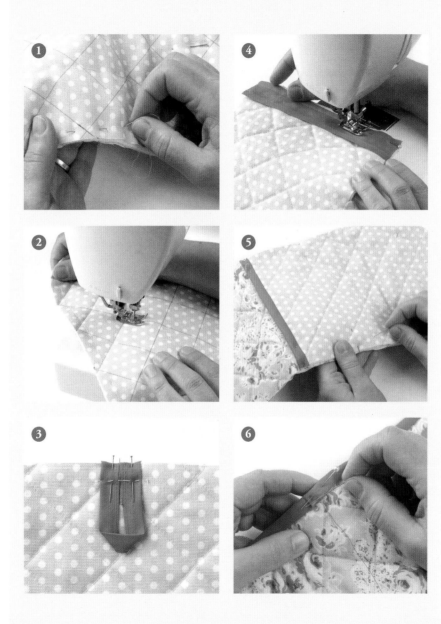

3 Take the shortest length of bias binding and fold in half lengthwise, wrong sides together. Stitch to join the two edges together. Fold the longest of the fabric pieces in half widthwise to find the center point and mark it on one edge with a pin on the main-fabric side. Take one end of the stitched length of binding and pin it to the edge of the fabric to the right of the marker pin, so the raw edges match and the stitching on the binding is next to the pin. Repeat with the other end of the binding to pin it to the left of the marker pin. Baste across the ends.

4 Take one 7" (18 cm) length of bias binding and use to bind the straight edge of one of the small pieces of fabric, using the slipstitch method (see page 51). Repeat with the second small fabric piece.

5 Pin one of the small pieces of fabric at each end of the longer piece, on the contrasting fabric side and baste to secure the edges.

6 Use the remaining length of binding to bind all around the edge of the oven mitt, trimming any excess binding to ¾" (2 cm) before overlapping the ends (see page 53).

BEADED QUILTED THROW

Essentially a simple coverlet made more interesting by using quilting and beading, it can be thrown over the bed for extra warmth on chilly nights, used as a bedspread over plainer sheets and blankets, or simply to snuggle up in. This traditional floral fabric has muted charm but a silky, satin-like material will add a touch more glamour.

Whichever style of fabric your choose, that for the back and front of the coverlet should be a closely woven, light- to mediumweight material. You can use the same material for both the front and back or choose two different fabrics, so you have one pattern on the front and another pattern, or plain, on the back. You also could use a piece of patchwork for a traditional country-style look.

The batting used for this quilt is curtain interlining – the slightly fleecy fabric that is used as an insulating layer in curtains.

Although the quilt here is trimmed with beading, other finishes would work well, such as a lace edging, ribbon, bobbles, or a ruffle of a lighter satiny material.

YOU WILL NEED

- Fabric – for amount see below

- Curtain interlining – for amount see below

- Basting and matching thread

- Erasable marker

- Beaded trim or other trim for three sides, optional

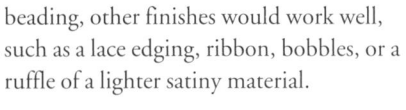

Decide on how big you want the final quilt and cut out two pieces of fabric to this size, plus ⅝" (1.5 cm) all around for the seam allowances. Cut out two pieces of curtain interlining to the same dimensions.

VARIATION

For a softer look, give the coverlet rounded corners. After cutting out the fabric and interlining, pin them together. Mark around the edge of a large dinner plate at the corners and trim (see page 21). At step 2, snip into the curved seam at the corners to reduce the bulk when the coverlet is turned to the right side.

1 Pin one piece of interlining to the wrong side of one piece of fabric. Secure with lines of basting, working outward from the center and then around the sides. Repeat with the other piece of interlining and fabric.

2 Pin the two pieces of fabric right sides together, and stitch around the sides, ⅝" (1.5 cm) from the edge and leaving a gap of about 12" (30 cm) in the center of one side. Trim the seam allowances to ⅜" (1 cm)

OPTIONS

Beads make an ideal finishing touch for this coverlet. At the end of step 1, baste the insertion tape of the beaded trim to the right side of the coverlet on two or three sides of the fabric, positioning the bottom edge of the insertion tape ⅝" (1.5 cm) below the fabric edge. Then make up the coverlet as described. When you turn the coverlet to the right side, the trim will be sandwiched in the seam.

and snip across the corners. Turn to the right side through the gap and then slipstitch the opening closed. Press around the edges.

3 Using an erasable marker, mark the quilting lines on one side of the coverlet (see pages 76–7). Baste across the quilt,

working outward from the center, through all the layers of fabric.

4 Hand or machine stitch along the quilting lines, working from the center out and finishing ⅝" (1.5 cm) from the outside edge then stitch all around the quilt, ⅝" (1.5 cm) in from the outside edge.

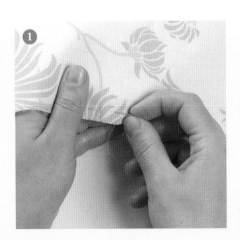

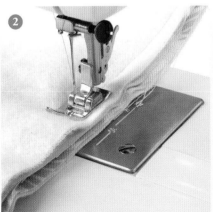

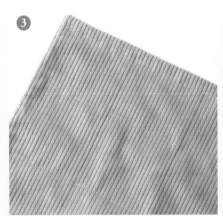

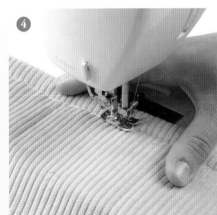

PADDED HEADBOARD

A padded covering slipped over an existing headboard is a great way to add comfort and style to your bedroom. This one has row of simple quilting to secure the padding and give it a decorative touch. A washable, hardwearing fabric is a practical choice, but you could choose something more sumptuous, such as silk or satin, or even fake fur or suede.

YOU WILL NEED

- Main fabric

- Lining fabric

- Mediumweight batting

- Six 16″ (40 cm) lengths of tape or ribbon for ties

- Basting and matching thread

- Erasable marker

Before you begin, take the mattress off the bed. Measure from the bottom of the headboard on one side, over the top and then back down to the bottom on the other side; this is **A**. Measure the width of the headboard, making sure you measure around the depth on one side; this is **B**. Cut out a piece of batting that is **A** plus 1¼" (3 cm) by **B** plus 2" (5 cm). Cut out a piece of main fabric and a piece of lining fabric the same size.

SHAPED HEADBOARD

To make a cover for a non-rectangular headboard, create a paper pattern the same shape that allows extra for the depth of the headboard and allowances. Use this to cut out two pieces of main fabric, two of lining and two of batting. Mark the pieces of main fabric as in step 1. Sandwich each piece of batting between main fabric and lining pieces. Baste as in step 1. Quilt each piece as desired. Pin the two pieces right sides together and stitch around the top and sides. Hem and add ties as in step 4.

1 Using an erasable marker, mark the quilting lines on the right side of the main fabric (see page 77). Sandwich the batting between the two pieces of fabric. Secure with lines of basting, working from the center outward and then around the sides. Hand or machine stitch along the quilting lines to secure the layers.

2 Fold the cover in half widthwise, right sides together; pin the sides. Stitch through all the layers, taking a ⅝" (1.5 cm) allowance. Trim the batting at the seam close to the stitching. Remove the basting.

3 Mark along the fold at the top of the cover with pins. Match the pins to one side seam, with the right sides of the main fabric facing. Pin across the top of the seam the measurement that is the depth of the headboard. Stitch as pinned. Trim the seam to a ⅝" (1.5 cm) allowance. Trim the batting at the seam close to the stitching. Repeat on the other side seam.

4 Turn up a 1½" (4 cm) hem at the lower edge. Sew in place with catchstitch (see page 11). Pin three ties, evenly spaced, to one side of the cover at the hem. Repeat on the other side of the cover. Stitch the ties in place. Turn the cover right side out. Fit it over the headboard. Tie the ties together under the headboard.

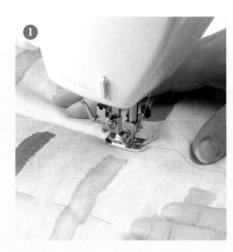

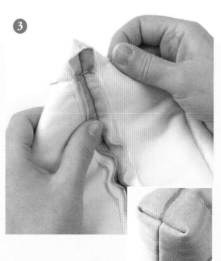

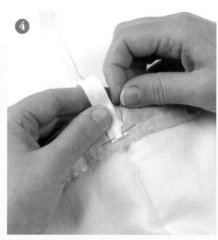

LINED LINEN BASKET

Banish wash-day blues with this pretty – and practical – laundry-basket liner. Wicker baskets look lovely and, being lightweight, are easy to carry. However, rough edges of wicker can catch delicate linens and garments. The simple solution is to make a fabric liner that fits inside the basket, covering any potential snags.

The ideal fabric for this project is a lightweight one; a material that's too stiff won't fit comfortably in the basket. Pick something with a close weave to help prevent rough pieces of the wicker piercing the fabric.

Begin this project by cutting out the fabric as follows. Put your basket onto a piece of paper and draw around the base. Set the basket aside and clean up the drawn line. Cut around this line to make the pattern and then use it to cut one piece of fabric for the base of the liner. Measure around the top of basket and add 1¼" (3 cm); measure the depth and add 1¼" (3 cm); then cut a piece of fabric to these dimensions for the sides of the liner. Measure from one handle to the other around the top of the basket and add on 1¼" (3 cm). Cut two bias strips this measurement by 6" (15 cm). Cut two lengths of lacy trim to this measurement, plus extra for turnings.

YOU WILL NEED

- Fabric – 2 yards (1.75 m) of 60" (150 cm) wide fabric is enough for a basket 24" (60 cm) long and 18" (45 cm) wide

- Lacy trim – 2 yards (1.5 m) for a basket of the given size

- Ribbon – 4 yards (3.5 m) for a basket of the given size

- Basting and matching threads

1 Fold the fabric side piece in half width-wise, right sides together. Pin and baste the short edges together, taking a ⅝" (1.5 cm) allowance. Put into the basket – the right side against the basket and ⅝" (1.5 cm) folded up at the base. Pin the fabric edge to the basket's edge. Fold the excess fabric inside the basket into pleats and secure with pins – hide the seam in one of the pleats.

2 When you are happy with the fit of the liner – don't make it too tight – take the liner out and baste the pleats in place. Machine stitch the pleats then zigzag along each allowance ⅜" (1 cm) from the stitching. Trim each allowance close to the zigzagging. Press the seams to one side.

3 Replace the liner in the basket; trim around the top to 1¼" (3cm) above the edge. Take the liner out and turn under ¼" (5 mm) around top edge; press. Turn under another ⅜" (1 cm); pin and press. Stitch all around. Pin the bottom edge of the sides to the edge of the base fabric, right sides together. (If your sides are too full, run gathering stitches around the bottom and use these to draw up the fabric.)

4 Baste and stitch the seam, taking a ⅝" (1.5 cm) allowance. Snip into the allowance for ease of fit then zigzag all around.

5 Turn under the short ends of each bias strip by ¼" (5 mm); press. Turn under another ⅜" (1 cm); pin, press and then stitch each turning. Turn under one long edge of each bias strip by ⅜" (1 cm); press. Pin the lacy trim along the allowance on one strip so that the part of the trim you want visible on the right side falls below the fold; pin through the allowance only and then baste where pinned.

6 Unfold the allowance on one strip and then machine stitch the trim in place, stitching ⅝" (1.5 cm) from the raw edge of the fabric. Turn the allowance back under and press again. Repeat on the other strip. Cut two pieces of ribbon, each one as long as a bias strip plus 35" (90 cm). Pin one ribbon along the lace-trimmed edge of one strip, ¼" (5 mm) from the fold of the fabric and so the center point of the ribbon matches the center point of the strip. Stitch along both sides of the ribbon. Repeat on the other bias strip.

7 Put the liner in the basket and hold in place with pins or tape. Pin the bias strips in position to the top of the liner, right sides together and matching the raw edge of the strip to the turned edge of the liner. Baste then stitch, making sure you stitch below the turned hem. Finish raw edges with zigzag stitch and press allowances toward the lace-trimmed edges.

BEACH ROLL

This handy summertime accessory will make idling by the pool or shore even more enjoyable. Made to fold down or roll up in a flash, it has a shoulder strap for hands-free carrying. Its integral pillow and towel lining are the perfect surfaces from which to bask in the rays of the sun.

YOU WILL NEED

- Main fabric 45 x 65" (115 x 165 cm), plus extra for the ties and shoulder strap ties (see steps 2 and 7 below)

- Toweling, 39½ x 59" (100 x 150 cm)

- Batting, ¾" (2 cm) thick, about 1 yard (1 meter)

Making up

1 Cut four pieces of batting, each 12 x 38½" (30 x 85 cm), for the padded section. Put the four pieces together and baste loosely together to hold. Position the batting at one end of the toweling fabric 3" (7.5 cm) down from the top edge and 3" (7.5 cm) from either side. Secure to the toweling with a few large, loose basting stitches.

2 Cut two lengths of main fabric, each 1½ x 45" (4 x 115 cm) for the ties. Make the ties, finishing off both ends (see page 37).

3 Now mark the positions for the ties. Using a pin and on the right side, mark a point 13" (32.5 cm) from one long edge of the fabric and 17¼" (44 cm) down from the top edge. Repeat on the opposite side of the fabric so you have two positions marked at one end of the fabric.

4 Fold one tie in half and press to make an obvious fold mark. Pin this tie to the fabric through this fold at one of the marked positions and then stitch in place along the fold line. Repeat with the other tie to stitch it in place.

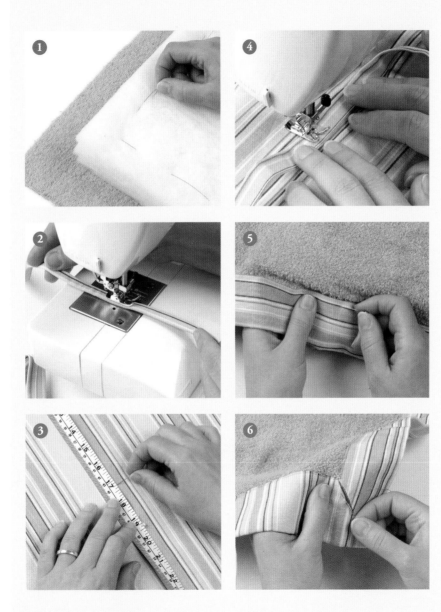

5 Turn under ⅝" (1.5 cm) around the edge of the fabric; press in place. Lay out the fabric flat, wrong side up, with the ties at the bottom. Center the toweling on top so the padded section is at the top of the fabric, with the batting on the underside. Fold the edges of the fabric up and over the edges of the towel, folding the fabric into miters at the corners. Pin in place and trim away any excess fabric at the corners.

6 Press and then topstitch all around the pinned edge of the fabric, making sure that you don't stitch through the ties. Then topstitch across the width of the towel, just bellow the edge of the padding – starting and finishing your stitching at the edge of the fabric border. Slipstitch the seams (see page 11) at the corners by hand.

7 Cut a length of main fabric 1½ x 41" (4 x 104 cm) and make into a tie, finishing off both ends (see page 37). Stitch one end 6¾" (17 cm) in from the outside edge and 6½" (16 cm) from the bottom edge, stitching though the main fabric. Stitch the other end the same distance in from the opposite edge and up from the bottom.

DINING CHAIR COVER

Give your dining room chairs a new look with a matching set of hand-made chair covers. These covers are easy to make and can be coordinated to your table linens or other soft furnishings. They fit over each chair and are secured with pretty ties at the front and back, so the chair beneath is completely concealed.

YOU WILL NEED

- Main fabric – for amount see below

- Lining – for amount see below

- Basting and matching thread

- Erasable fabric marker

- Paper, pencil, and masking tape

MAKING THE PATTERN

Lay one long panel of paper over the chair, joining pieces of paper as necessary, so that the paper touches the ground at the back of the chair and at the front, and follows the shape of the chair. Trim the paper to fit as necessary. Tape pieces of paper to the sides of the seat and then cut to fit the sides of the chair. Don't trim the pattern too close to the chair at any point, as you will need some give in the finished cover. Using a pencil, mark the positions where you want the ties to be on the finished cover.

Using the pattern as a guide, transfer the marks that indicate the positions of the ties to the right side of the lining fabric.

1 Create your pattern (see left). For each chair, use the pattern to cut out one piece of lining fabric and one piece of main fabric, adding ⅝" (1.5 cm) all around and 1¼" (3 cm) along the bottom of the back for allowances and ease of fit. Using an erasable fabric marker, transfer the marks for the ties from the pattern (see left) to the right side of the lining fabric. Cut out eight lengths of fabric, each 2¼ x 12" (5.5 x 30 cm) for the ties.

2 Make the ties, finishing one end of each (see page 37). Lay out the lining fabric right side up. Pin a tie at each marked point, matching the raw end of each tie to the raw edge of the fabric. Baste each one in place.

3 Take the lining fabric and bring the edges that fall along the front legs of the chair right sides together; pin and stitch. Repeat with the main fabric. Snip into the fold at the top of each seam and then press the seams open.

4 Put the lining and main fabric pieces right sides together and pin all around. Machine stitch around the edge, leaving a 10" (25 cm) gap in the bottom edge of the chair back. Turn the chair cover to the right side through the gap, then slipstitch the gap closed; press.

5 Place the chair cover over your chair, making sure the ties align. Tie the ties together to secure.

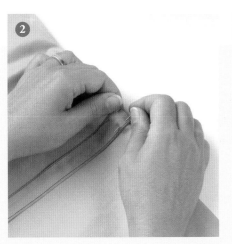

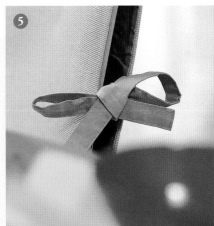

Fabric glossary

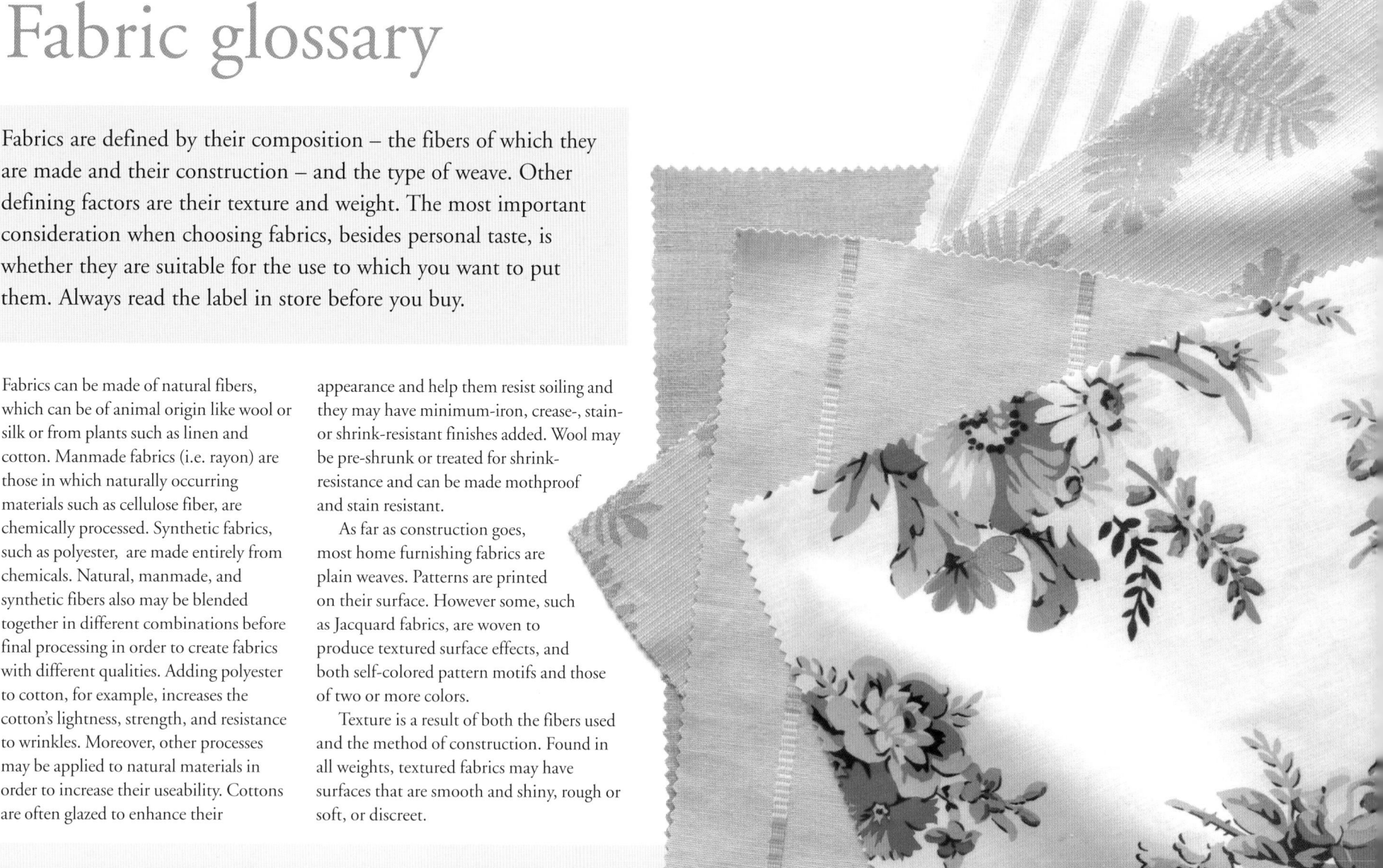

Fabrics are defined by their composition – the fibers of which they are made and their construction – and the type of weave. Other defining factors are their texture and weight. The most important consideration when choosing fabrics, besides personal taste, is whether they are suitable for the use to which you want to put them. Always read the label in store before you buy.

Fabrics can be made of natural fibers, which can be of animal origin like wool or silk or from plants such as linen and cotton. Manmade fabrics (i.e. rayon) are those in which naturally occurring materials such as cellulose fiber, are chemically processed. Synthetic fabrics, such as polyester, are made entirely from chemicals. Natural, manmade, and synthetic fibers also may be blended together in different combinations before final processing in order to create fabrics with different qualities. Adding polyester to cotton, for example, increases the cotton's lightness, strength, and resistance to wrinkles. Moreover, other processes may be applied to natural materials in order to increase their useability. Cottons are often glazed to enhance their

appearance and help them resist soiling and they may have minimum-iron, crease-, stain- or shrink-resistant finishes added. Wool may be pre-shrunk or treated for shrink-resistance and can be made mothproof and stain resistant.

As far as construction goes, most home furnishing fabrics are plain weaves. Patterns are printed on their surface. However some, such as Jacquard fabrics, are woven to produce textured surface effects, and both self-colored pattern motifs and those of two or more colors.

Texture is a result of both the fibers used and the method of construction. Found in all weights, textured fabrics may have surfaces that are smooth and shiny, rough or soft, or discreet.

Barkweave A self-colored fabric with a rough texture similar to that of tree bark. It is generally made from cotton.

Brocade A medium- or heavyweight fabric with a raised pattern. The patterns are often formed by metallic threads.

Broderie Anglaise A white or pale pastel colored lightweight cotton fabric with a lacy embroidered pattern and cut-out detail. Generally available as a trimming.

Buckram This is usually made from cotton or jute and is used with other fabrics as stiffening. It comes in several different weights. Washing may remove some of the stiffening.

Burlap Usually made from jute, this is a strong, coarse, and loosely woven fabric that is hardwearing and informal. It may sag when draped.

Calico Plain-woven cotton that comes in a range of weights and qualities depending on the yarn used. Can be bought pre-shrunk or un-shrunk, and bleached and unbleached.

Cambric A fine, plain-woven cotton or linen fabric, it usually has a glaze on the right side that adds stiffening. A

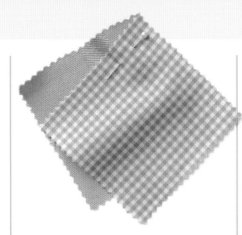

down-proof form is used as a permanent inner cover for pillows and quilts.

Canvas A heavyweight, closely woven, cotton or linen that is informal and hardwearing. Sometimes known as duck.

Chambray A lightweight but hardwearing cotton fabric. Generally, the warp threads of this material are colored, whereas the weft threads are white. It has a denim-like appearance and is most commonly available in shades of blue.

Chenille A medium- to heavyweight cotton or cotton/synthetic blend with a soft pile.

Chiffon A very sheer, plain weave fabric made in cotton, silk, or synthetic fibers.

Chintz A plain-weave, mediumweight cotton with a glazed surface, that is usually printed with floral patterns.

Corduroy Hardwearing, medium- to heavyweight fabric, usually cotton, with a ridged pile. The ribs can vary from very wide to narrow needlecord.

Crêpe This is a fine, lightweight fabric, with a slightly crinkled surface, which can be made from cotton, wool, silk, or synthetic fibers.

Curtain interlining Used inside curtains to add warmth; Domette is a lightweight interlining, whereas bump is thicker.

Curtain lining This is usually a closely woven, cotton sateen, a fabric with a slight sheen. It comes in a range of colors, though is most usually sold in white or shades of cream.

Damask Made on a Jacquard loom so that the threads form an unraised floral or geometric design against a satin-weave ground. Similar to but finer than brocade.

Denim A hardwearing, mediumweight cotton fabric with a twill weave. The warp threads are usually a dark blue and the weft are generally white.

Dimity A sheer cotton that uses heavier threads to create a pattern in the weave.

Dobby weave Any fabric where the weave produces a small, raised geometric pattern.

Dotted Swiss A sheer cotton with a woven pattern of opaque dots.

Drill A hardwearing, mediumweight, closely woven cotton with a twill weave.

Dupioni Medium- to heavyweight, silk or synthetic fabric with a distinctive slubbed surface on one side.

Fake fur Synthetic fabric with fibers that simulate real fur.

Fake suede A plain-weave cotton or synthetic fabric that has been given a slight nap on one side to resemble the texture of real suede.

Felt A non-woven, mediumweight fabric that can be made of almost any fiber. It doesn't fray when cut.

Flannel A soft, lightweight fabric with either a plain or twill weave. It has a slight nap and can be made with cotton, wool, or synthetic fibers.

Fleece A modern synthetic fabric with the texture of a lightweight wool fleece.

Gabardine A light- to mediumweight, hardwearing cotton or wool with a twill weave.

Gingham A plain-weave, light- to mediumweight checked or striped cotton or cotton/synthetic blend in two colors. The checks or stripes come in a range of sizes and shades.

Interfacing This is used to stiffen other fabrics. You can use a fusible interfacing that is ironed on, or a sewn-on variety. Both come in a wide range of different weights.

Jacquard weave This is any fabric where the weave produces a raised pattern (such as damask or brocade).

Jersey A lightweight, plain-knit fabric made from wool, cotton, silk, or synthetic fibers, or a blend.

Lace An openwork, lightweight fabric in cotton or synthetic fibers. A wide range of lace trimmings is also available.

Lawn A very fine, semi-sheer cotton or cotton blend with a smooth, even surface.

Linen A hardwearing fabric made from the flax plant that ranges from very fine to heavyweight but with a tendency to crease.

Linen union A mediumweight, linen and cotton blend.

Madras A plain-weave, lightweight cotton in strongly colored plaids, stripes, or checks.

Moiré Any fabric finished with a water-marked effect. It's generally associated with silk taffeta, but can be made with cotton or synthetic fibers. Light- to mediumweight.

Muslin This plain-weave cotton comes in a range of weights and qualities, bleached or unbleached. The sheer, loosely woven, very lightweight muslin is the most popularly used. Swiss muslin has decorative embroidered detail.

Nap A fabric with a nap has short fibers on the surface that have been drawn out of the yarn of the fabric.

Net A very lightweight, sheer fabric with an open mesh, made in cotton or synthetic fibers.

Organdy A sheer, plain-weave fabric, usually cotton, that has been stiffened slightly.

Organza A thin, transparent silk or synthetic that is slightly stiff.

Ottoman Medium- to heavyweight, hardwearing fabric with a horizontal rib, made from wool, cotton, silk, or synthetic fibers.

Plain weave Any fabric where the weft thread goes under one and then over one warp thread.

Percale A lightweight cotton or cotton-blend fabric with a fine, plain weave, that's often used for bed linen.

Pile fabrics Any fabric that resembles fur to some degree, in that it has raised fibers that obscure the basic weave of the fabric. Fake fur, terrycloth, corduroy, and velvet are all pile fabrics.

Polished cotton Any cotton with a glazed finish.

Poplin A fabric where the weft threads are slightly heavier than the warp, giving a slight ribbed effect. It can be made from most fiber types but is most commonly found in a medium- to heavyweight cotton.

PVC coated A polyvinyl chloride topcoat is applied to a woven or knitted fabric so that a tough, non-porous fabric is produced. This can be wiped clean.

Repp A fabric with a ribbed effect, such as ottoman.

Sateen A cotton fabric woven with the same type of weave used for silk or synthetic satin to create a light- to mediumweight fabric with a subtle sheen.

Satin A silk or synthetic fabric created with a satin weave to produce a smooth and slippery fabric. It comes in a wide range of weights.

Satin weave Any fabric where the weft threads pass over more than one and then under one warp thread, giving the fabric a lustrous sheen.

Seersucker A mediumweight cotton or cotton blend with a crinkly texture in the weave. It is usually striped or checked.

Serge A hardwearing, mediumweight wool, silk, or synthetic fabric with a twill weave.

Shantung A lightweight fabric with an uneven, slubbed texture. Usually silk but it can also be cotton or synthetic.

Sheeting Plain-weave cotton, linen, or polyester/cotton mix fabric of a weight suitable for sheets and another bedlinen. Available in larger than average width and in a range of colors and patterns.

Suiting Any fabric that could be used to make suits or coats.

Taffeta A mediumweight, slightly shiny fabric with a crisp finish. It can be made with silk, cotton, or synthetic fibers.

Terrycloth A cotton fabric with a nap of uncut loops on one or both sides that is commonly used for towels and washcloths.

Ticking A mediumweight drill cloth that is traditionally striped.

Tweed A heavyweight woollen fabric with a rough texture that is usually checked or plaid.

Twill Any fabric where the weave has created diagonal ridges on the surface of the material (such as gabardine, serge, or drill).

Union A name give to fabrics that consist of mixed fiber in the yarn or cloth. Cotton and linen unions are robust and hardwearing.

Velour A warm, heavy fabric with a thick pile. Can be made of cotton, wool, or synthetic fibers.

Velvet A pile fabric made from cotton, silk, or synthetic blends – the pile may be made from one fiber while the backing is made from another. It's a medium- to heavyweight fabric.

Velveteen A cotton pile fabric that is very similar to velvet and which comes in a variety of weights. It has a slightly duller sheen than velvet

Voile A soft, sheer fabric made from loosely woven cotton or synthetic yarn.

Worsted A combed wool yarn or woolen fabric that is hardwearing but has a smooth surface texture.

Appliqué 64–5, 69
Apron 58–9
Backstitch 10, 11
Basting 10, 11
Beach roll 88–9
Beaded quilted throw 82–3
Bias binding 50–53
Bias loops, making 37
Blanket stitch 10, 11
Bobbin case 13
Bobbin winder 13
Bodkin 8
Buttonholes, making by hand 35
Buttons 34–5
   sewing on 35
Catchstitch 10, 11
Children's tepee 46–7
Clothespin bag 56–7
Cube 42–3
Curves, making 21
Curtains
   café 70–71
   eyelet 62–3
   tab-top 26–7
Cushions
   bolster 30–31
   simple 22–3
Diaper stacker 60
Dining chair cover 90–91
Duffel bag 68–9
Duvet cover 40–41

Enlarging a design 21
Equipment 8–9 see also individual items
Eyelet curtains 62–3
Fabric
   amounts 7
   cutting 7
   glossary 92–5
   grain of 7
   know-how 6–7
Hand finishing 17
Hand stitches 10–11
Handwheel 13
Headboard, padded 84–5
Hem stitch 10, 11
Hems 18–19
   basic double 19
   basic single 19
   blanket-stitched 19
   hand-rolled 19
Lined linen basket 86–7
Lining, quilting and 76–7
Loops 36, 37
Mini beanbag 72–3
Mitered corners 32–3
Needle clamp 13
Needle threader 8
Oven mitts 80–81
Overhand stitch 10
Padded headboard 84–5
Padding 77
Pattern(s)

and scaling 20–21
   cutting out a 21
   enlarging a 21, 57
   using a 21
Pin cushion 8
Pins and needles 8
Piping 54–5
Placemats 78–9
Pocket storage 48–9
Polybeads, working with 73
Presser foot 13
Quilting techniques 76–7, 80, 82
Rickrack 70–71
Roll-up shade 44–5
Ruffles 66
Running stitch 10, 11
Scaling, patterns and 20–21
Scissors 9
Seam allowance 16
Seam ripper 8
Seams 16–17
   flat fell 17
   French 17
   mock French 17
   plain 17
   self-finished 17
   topstitched 17
Sewing machine
   basics 12–15
   correcting tension 14
   feet 15

finishing 14
   getting started 14
   stitch length 15
   stitches 15
Shears 9
Slipstitch 10, 11, 51
Snaps 36
Spool pin 13
Stitch length selector 13
Straight stitch 15
Tablecloths 28–9
Table runners 24–5
Tabs 36, 37
Tab-top curtains 26–7
Take-up lever 13
Tape measure 9
Tension guide 13
Tension settings 13
Thimble 8
Thread cutter 13
Threads 8
Throat plate 13
Ties 36, 37
Topstitch 15
Tote bag 74–5
Trims, using 66–7
Velcro® 37, 45
Zigzag stitch 15
Zippers 38–9
   sewing in 39
   shortening a 39